# lessons from the
# future

# STAN DAVIS

# lessons from the

# future

## making sense of a blurred world

### FROM THE WORLD'S LEADING FUTURIST

CAPSTONE

First published 2001 by
Capstone Publishing Ltd (A John Wiley & Sons Co.)
8 Newtec Place
Magdalen Road
Oxford OX4 1RE
United Kingdom
http://www.capstoneideas.com

British Library Cataloguing in Publication Data
A CIP catalogue record for this book is available from the British Library

ISBN 1-84112-070-7

Typeset by
Forewords, 109 Oxford Road, Cowley, Oxford
Printed and bound by
T.J. International Ltd, Padstow, Cornwall

This book is printed on acid-free paper

*To the memory of my father*
*David Davis*
*(1911–1999)*

# Contents

# Acknowledgements

The author and publishers wish to thank the following for permission to use copyright material:

Chapter 1: from *Future Perfect* by Stan Davis, Copyright © 1996 Stanley M. Davis. Reprinted by permission of Addison-Wesley Publishing Co., Inc.

Chapter 2: from *2020 Vision* by Stan Davis and Bill Davidson. Copyright © 1991 William Davidson and Stanley M. Davis. Reprinted by permission of Simon & Schuster, Inc.

Chapter 3: from *BLUR* by Stan Davis and Christopher Meyer. Copyright © 1998 Stanley M. Davis and Christopher Meyer. Reprinted by Permission of Perseus Books.

Chapter 4: from "We're Already Surrounded by Them . . ." by Stan Davis, *Forbes ASAP*, 1 June 1998. Reprinted by permission of FORBES Magazine, Forbes Inc.

Chapter 5: from *Future Wealth* by Stan Davis and Christopher Meyer. Copyright © 2000 Stanley M. Davis and Ernst & Young

LLP. Reprinted by permission of the Harvard Business School Press.

Chapter 6: from *Future Wealth* by Stan Davis and Christopher Meyer. Copyright © 2000 Stanley M. Davis and Ernst & Young LLP. Reprinted by permission of the Harvard Business School Press.

Chapter 8: from *2020 Vision* by Stan Davis and Bill Davidson. Copyright © 1991 William Davidson and Stanley M. Davis. Reprinted by permission of Simon & Schuster, Inc.

Chapter 9: from *The Monster Under the Bed* by Stan Davis and Jim Botkin. Copyright © 1994 Stanley M. Davis and James Botkin. Reprinted by permission of Simon & Schuster, Inc.

Chapter 10: from "What's Your Emotional Bandwidth" by Stan Davis, *Forbes*, 7 July 1997. Reprinted by permission of FORBES Magazine, Forbes Inc.

Chapter 11: from *Future Perfect* by Stan Davis, Copyright © 1996 Stanley M. Davis. Reprinted by permission of Addison-Wesley Publishing Co., Inc.

Chapter 12: from *BLUR* by Stan Davis and Christopher Meyer. Copyright © 1998 Stanley M. Davis and Christopher Meyer. Reprinted by Permission of Perseus Books.

Chapter 13: from "Business Wins, Organization Kills" by Stan Davis, *Forbes ASAP*, 7 April 1997. Reprinted by permission of FORBES Magazine, Forbes Inc.

Chapter 14: from *Future Wealth* by Stan Davis and Christopher Meyer. Copyright © 2000 Stanley M. Davis and Ernst & Young LLP. Reprinted by permission of the Harvard Business School Press.

Chapter 15: from "Three Vice Presidents in Mid-Life" by Stan Davis and Roger Gould, *Harvard Business Review*, July–August 1981. Reprinted by permission of Harvard Business School Press.

Chapter 16: from *Managing Corporate Culture* by Stan Davis. Copyright © 1984 Stanley M. Davis.

Chapter 17: from *Matrix* by Stanley M. Davis and Paul R. Lawrence. Copyright © 1977 Stanley M. Davis and Paul R. Lawrence. Reprinted by permission of Addison-Wesley Publishing Co., Inc.

Chapter 18: from "What Will Replace the Tech Economy" by Stanley M. Davis. May 2000. Copyright © 2000 Time Inc. Reprinted by permission of Time Life Syndication.

Chapter 20: from *2020 Vision* by Stan Davis and Bill Davidson. Copyright © 1991 William Davidson and Stanley M. Davis. Reprinted by permission of Simon & Schuster, Inc.

The publishers have made every effort to trace copyright-holders. If any have been inadvertently overlooked the publishers will be pleased to make the necessary arrangement at the first opportunity.

# Preface

With a Ph.D. in the social sciences, I spent the first twenty years of my career at the Harvard Business School and other universities. Then, starting in the early 1980s, I became a "free agent" writer, consultant, and public speaker. The marketplace labelled me a "futurist," that peculiar breed of thinker who anticipates the changes sweeping through society and identifies the business opportunities they present.

In a 1987 book called *Future Perfect*, I coined the term "mass customization" and introduced the business world to the importance of an anytime, anyplace orientation. In my 1991 book, *2020 Vision*, I described the coming shift from the first to second half of the information economy, and predicted its end in the late 2020s – a prediction I still claim. Three years later, in *The Monster Under the Bed*, I stressed the importance of knowledge-based businesses, and in the 1998 best-seller, *BLUR*, I emphasized the convergence of speed, connectivity, and intangibles in the marketplace. In my most recent book, *Future Wealth*, I focus on the shift in the control of wealth away from big organizations and to the individual.

I was flattered when Capstone Publishing asked me to retrace my thinking, assemble my past and present work, and add some current thoughts. This is a perilous task for someone who writes about the future, and I was reminded of the quip about the physically challenged futurist who saw far ahead but just a little off to the side. While surely I do not see all that lies ahead, I am blessed with the confidence that I have been largely right about what I do sense.

I have selected writings for this volume whose truth and impact generally still lie in the future, because many of these predictions are still playing themselves out. I have included some new pieces as well. What you will read here is the evolution of one thinker about what I and others call the new, networked or connected economy. I hope you enjoy them as much as I have enjoyed thinking this through and capturing those ideas in print.

# Part I

Ideas

# How I get my ideas

I am often asked "How do you come up with your ideas?," and have long wanted to capture some thoughts on how to think about the future and pass them on to others in the hope that they work for you. This introduction seems like a good place to do just that. I also want this volume to be about how to generate ideas.

You might ask, when you make a prediction, how do you know you are going to be right? How do you avoid being that peripheral futurist? One guide I have long used is this:

"Life is complex, the truth is simple."

Of all the lines I have written, this is my favourite. I wrote it about 15 years ago and never published it. It has always been my touchstone for knowing if I had it right about anything. It says to me that if something is complex to you, you are not yet at the truth of it. When you are at the truth, there is an ease and clarity and it seems simple. I have found this a wonderful signpost through the years, for personal as well as professional decisions. It is a great aid for problem solving and for gauging the future accurately.

For me, "Are you right about what you did say?" is more important than "Did you get it all?" Like all of us who study the future, I miss lots of what is coming. In 1991, for example, I accurately predicted the shift to the second half of the information age within a few years yet, like just about everyone else at that time, missed foreseeing the internet as the specific vehicle.

One way of increasing accuracy in prediction, and a "top tip" for wannabe futurists, is to focus on discovery and eschew invention. I admire inventors greatly. They are true creators of something out of nothing. Entrepreneurs are brilliant this way. Discovering the future, however, is a far less amazing skill than inventing it. The thing discovered already exists; you simply see it before most others do. Often it is a new piece of technology that makes it possible for something to happen on a large scale. So, find a direction things are moving in and spell out the ultimate logic or conclusion. If you are right there will be early examples of the thing already around. You are not creating the trend, you are simply spotting it before others.

Churn, for example, is increasing in the number of companies people work for in their careers. It has gone from one or two to ten or fifteen jobs within a few decades. Today, it is far more common to only stay with a company for a few years and to move up by moving on. What is the ultimate logic? How much more churn has to occur before you get who you are really working for. The answer, of course, is yourself. Once you make that discovery, you are no longer an employee, you are a free agent. This is partly why we predict a day when "The *Wall Street Journal* reports that 45 percent of the American workforce are free agents" (see p. 60). Then you search for more supportive evidence and related developments, such as boundaries are more permeable and alliances replace integrated stand-alone companies, and people change companies more and more frequently.

The simplicity and discovery rules are two specific ways I come up with ideas. It is also clear to me that self-taught skills matter more than native intelligence. Here, I have to be autobiographical. My career had two major turning points, which led to different tracks, each travelled for two decades, first as an academic and then as a free agent.

My undergraduate degree was in the social sciences, with a strong emphasis on what was then called "intellectual history" or "the history of ideas". It was the late 1950s to early 1960s and I studied under many great thinkers, several of whom were European refugees from the Second World War and steeped in the great books of antiquity. When I got to graduate school, however, instead of big thoughts and theory I was schooled in little thoughts and researchable hypotheses about testable variables. Boring, but I got my union card. Now I could teach.

My first career crisis was what to do with my degrees. At the time, my entire professional self-image was tied up in becoming a professor. I wanted to be an educator, but I could not see myself spending 40 years in what looked like a pretty dry field. I resolved to switch out of the school of arts and sciences and to teach at a professional school, just by happenstance the Harvard Business School. I thought that a professional school (and it could as easily have been in education, government, or law) would be more real world, yet at the same time let me stay focused on ideas.

This worked for many years, then that pond also dried up. It was ironic and sad. I felt I had to leave academic life to stay intellectually alive. Can you believe that? I felt like a prodigal son for a long time. The transition from professor to free agent took seven years to complete, gradually turning my moonlighting into the whole of my work.

Only on the far side did I make a great discovery: I did not have to be an academic to be an educator. I am still an educator, I still write books and educate people from many public podiums. However, now I write trade books, not textbooks. These have been much more interesting than the texts – for both me and my readers – and they have reached a much wider audience.

These two career changes, from the arts and sciences to a professional school and then from academic to free agent, had major impacts on how I think. While you go through such changes, it is very painful to abandon one way and evolve another. However, on the far side it is generally worthwhile (see pp. 147–60). One thing it certainly does is teach you to trust yourself. You become your own person. You become more conscious about the choices you make, including which questions you are going to ask in your work, which ideas and problems you are going to pursue, and what to stop examining. It is not that you are any brighter or have more freedom, it is that you act more intentionally.

I know it has changed my source kit, evolved over 40 years, and which I offer to you here. I simply want to show you what works for me, in the hope that some of it will also work for you. The sources come in three basic flavors, and I give them each equal weight, importance, and time: reading, discussions, and thinking.

# Reading

I am not very systematic when I choose what to read. In chronological order of when I read them, some books that influenced me the most are *Paidea: The Ideals of Greek Culture* by Werner Jaeger; *The Federalist Papers: A History of Political Theory* by George Sabine; *The Last Temptation of Christ* by Nikos Kazantzakis; *One Hundred Years of Solitude* by Gabriel Garcia Marques; *Strategy and Structure* by Alfred Chandler; *Management* by Peter Drucker; *The Structure of Scientific Revolutions* by Thomas Kuhn; *The Dancing Wu Li Masters* by Gary Zukav; *Bionomics* by Michael Rothschild; and *Out of Control* by Kevin Kelly.

Serendipity plays as much of a role as do scans of tables of contents and search engines. I read as much outside my field as I do inside, let us say 50–50. Within the work focus, this divides about equally into four parts: books, newspapers, magazines, and articles that come to me individually through others and through searches. I probably read parts of three dozen business books a year, but only finish about one of these a month. I selectively read three papers daily (*Boston Globe, New York Times,* and *Wall Street Journal*) and several business magazines (*Business Week, The Economist, Fast Company, Forbes, Fortune, Red Herring, Wired*). Outside my field, I read mainly science/technology and fiction.

# Discussions

Discussions can occur with anyone, but over the years I have found several sources particularly rich.

One is a small research team that buys into the excitement of the topic and whose quality of mind is more important than their training or experience. Six of my last ten books, for example, were written in collaboration with a colleague. The last two and another that is in the pipeline involve working with a team.

A second route is a few close friends from other fields who love to talk about ideas. Chris Meyer, an economist with Cap Gemini Ernst & Young, fits both categories and has been a particularly close partner in ideas with me for a decade.

A third path is interactions with experts in a field that is new to me. I find this particularly useful when I have the kernel of an idea but need to work it out more clearly. Examples over time have been in information technology, robotics, nanotechnology, genomics, and investment banking. I generally begin with a brief description of my thinking and thesis and then go right to an open-ended "Tell me about what you do, about the new developments in your field, and how you see them relate to my topic." The best interviews are generally open explorations of ideas and not ones that make sure to cover a long list of questions. I prefer to look for a nugget or a switch that turns on and then probe it. I find this is a great way to climb a learning curve.

A fourth approach is to start talking about the idea on lots of public platforms. While I do a lot of public speaking around the world and address tens of thousands of people annually, I find this more important for articulation of the ideas than for creating them. My speeches have a content turnover of about one-third or more per year, so this is an excellent way of developing new material. You have to have the general thesis and basic idea, but it is in speaking to an audience that you can spontaneously work out the particulars. I find it akin to improv theater.

I have learned never to read a speech. Know the few main points you want to make, know where you will be for every five-minute interval, and have lots of examples. Some case-like examples come from the research, reading, and discussions. Audiences always know their specialty or industry better than you do, so it helps to give them an idea with a few examples and then ask them for one or two supporting examples from their field. This helps build your case and gets people involved. Of course, size and room set-up determine whether this is possible.

When I am lucky, a simple example portrays a serious idea. A current example that I particularly like is when I am trying to explain how technology is causing power to migrate from the center to the periphery, from the provider to the consumer. During one speech, I found myself saying, "How many of you have lawns? Who decides when the lawn gets watered?" (you do, even if you do so by setting the timer). Then I said, "Who should decide?" And, in unison, the audiences respond, "The lawn." Cheap and simple chip technology, spread around a lawn, only has to differentiate between wet/dry and turn water on/off. It is a clear and easy way to make a basic point.

From there you can go to lots of other examples: hot/cold, full/empty, here/gone of how things will increasingly get fast, cheap and out of control. If you have got time, it is fun to toss out one of those couplets, ask for examples, and dream up others that should happen or to name an object (door, chair, toilet) and ask "What would you want it to know and decide on its own?"

If power migrating to the periphery is a basic phenomenon, we should be able to find examples of it in our everyday life. Another important example of it came from my niece. Pregnant in her late thirties, she and her husband decided to have an amniocentesis to see if the fetus was all right. The doctor said "fine," but then she asked the following question: "By the way, how many of these have you performed and what has been your success rate?" The doctor looked at her and said, "I won't take you as a patient."

In microcosm, this is the confrontation between the old and coming order in medicine. "Who are patients to question doctors?" is the old approach, but now power is migrating from their top-down control and into the hands of their customers. We can expect these kinds of ratings to be routinely posted on a hospital's web page within the decade. Similarly, a few decades ago professors gave students grades and did not expect or tolerate being graded themselves, but today that is routine.

A fifth way that discussions help is through attending conferences, whether or not you are speaking at them. Here, as most of you surely know, conversations outside the meeting rooms provide half the value. Good speakers, however, can truly enrich your ideas. The day I wrote this, in fact, I heard two such speeches, one by Chuck D, leader and co-founder of the legendary rap group Public Enemy, and the other by the retired chief executive officer of CitiGroup, Walter Wriston.

Chuck D spoke eloquently about the battle over intellectual property caused by Napster and MP3 software. He argued persuasively that the lawsuits by major music companies are less about copyright and property rights and more about an entrenched oligarchy's futile attempt to keep control limited to the rich and powerful few. Technology not political demonstration is bringing both entrepreneurial opportunity and power to the periphery, to the artist and the people. The threat is less theft of intellectual property than it is change to the established business model. I think he is right.

By the end of this decade there will be more artists not fewer and more creativity not less. Technology has created a confrontation between oligarchy and democracy. This next wave will not wipe out the major studios any more than did the previous wave of independent studios. However, it will create a third tier, where microfocused creators and consumers of content will use the Internet to search each other out and connect. The majors will continue to serve the mass market, while the new tier will disintermediate the power structure and create huge entrepreneuial opportunities at the bottom. Each sentence in this paragraph has a researchable idea and presents several entrepreneurial opportunities.

When Chuck D handed over the podium to Wriston, the photographer snapped a photo of the young rapper in combat fatigues shaking hands with the retired banking giant, who chuckled, "Now my status will finally go up with my 19 year old grandson."

Wriston spoke forcefully about measurement. Measurements in the physical world took decades to be accepted and the metric system is still not widely used in the USA. Measurement changes in business and government will take even longer to be accepted. The world is changing at a much faster rate than are measurements. Pounds per square inch and revolutions per minute were once good indexes, but no more. The growing gap between book value and market cap points to a similar shift. Business has been particularly slow in addressing the need to measure intangibles, particularly intellectual capital.

Alongside traditional national and corporate accounts, we need to give equal importance to new measurements: the number of patents, prior filings, licensing and their income streams, the number of hours of training and percentage of employees being trained, the growth in education and amount of employee turnover, the rate of new product introduction, and the percentage of operations using six sigma guidelines. However, Wriston pessimistically predicted that such measures would not be on the balance sheet within the lifetime of the youngest person in the room. Measuring intangible economic value is an important field, worthy of more attention.

These were two hours well spent and major fuel for ideas about important issues.

## Thinking

My third major source of ideas is the not-so-prosaic task of thinking. Sometimes this means trying to solve a problem and sometimes figuring out what is the right focus or question and how to know when you have got it. It sounds pretentious, but it is important.

I am always struck about the importance of *how* to think when I listen to really bright people. They always seem to zero in on basic and powerful approaches, and avoid the trivial and derivative stuff. A business example is the difference between people with an idea for a start-up and those who do not explore ideas for start-ups unless they are capable of serving over a $1 billion marketplace.

The trick is knowing how to go for the big idea and I do not pretend to have *the* answer.

When I was young I spent a lot of time mastering my chosen field. First, I got the basics, then I built up a lot of knowledge on top of it. This is a good and necessary process. By mid-career I too often found myself working away at a piece of minutia in that pile of knowledge. That is when you have to switch your model.

This happened to me as a teacher. For 16 years I focused on preparing my classes and on bringing the best content possible to my students. One day it struck me that I was approaching things from the wrong end and I switched from watching what I was teaching to watching what they were learning. In business we know this as the difference between a product focus and a market focus. Whether on a speaking platform or alone at my keyboard, I find you will derive your best ideas when you strip away non-essentials and stay focused on the basics. Less is more.

In one of my first research interviews, I asked a senior executive what he worried about most on his job? I have never forgotten his answer: "What I worry about most is what we do not know that we do not know. What we know we do not know, we work very hard to get answers and solutions to. But what we do not know we do not know, we do not have a prayer or a chance at. My job," he said, "is moving people from not knowing what they do not know to knowing what they do not know. They take it from there." In today's lingo we talk about creative ideas as content. Given the current pace of change, however, we would do well to be context creators like that executive.

I like to put forth simple notions expressed in everyday language, find the more conceptual context, and iterate back and forth between the two. One notion that has served me very well for years, for example, is "Everything that has a beginning has an ending." I find this truism a rich source. I often use it as a starting point. From there I might go to "that means it has a life cycle" and I ask where are we in the life cycle of whatever it is we are examining, a concept, a technology, an economy. Or I might go to "what causes an ending?" In biology, for example, it seems that cells can only replicate and replace themselves a finite number of times, whereas species more often end because of externalities; they cannot adapt to changed circumstances and threats. Whatever your starting point, find a statement that grounds you, that you can take as axiomatic and return to it when you have gone as far as you can and need another start.

Most prophetic for me was the notion that the current economy would end in the late 2020s, a life cycle of approximately 75 years. The time was 1990, before the Internet took off. I had a starting point for the information economy in the early 1950s, because that is when gross domestic product and employment in industrial manufacturing reached its highest percentage. I read an advertisement that said half the homes in the USA would be able to connect their computers through their telephones by the mid-1990s/and I knew I had my mid-point. The economy's halfway mark would occur when computers went from freestanding machines to connected ones, "from crunching to connecting".

I thought, well, we have a starting time in the mid-1950s and a mid-point in the mid-1990s, so then how long before the end of the information economy? The industrial economy lasted from the 1760s to the 1950s, with the early infrastructure dominated by the steam engine and railroads and the late part driven by the internal combustion engine and cars. The second "half" was considerably shorter than the first. The same thing will be true for the information era, I reasoned, suggesting that it would last into the 2020s. That was the birth of my *2020 Vision*.

Taking the idea further, economies do not end because they run out of whatever is driving them. The dominance of one foundation ends because another more powerful one arrives. From agriculture to industry to information. What is next is biotechnology and, more specifically, genomics. Modern biotechnology began with Crick and Watson's discovery of the double helix structure of DNA in 1953 and gestated for almost five decades until completion of the Human Genome Project in June 2000. Now begins the second, growth quarter of this next economy and, by sometime during the late 2020s, it will have become powerful and pervasive enough to become the dominant foundation for the economy.

The increased pace of change is apparent everywhere and provides another example of how to mine ideas by starting with basics. Two years ago I was thinking about measurement and how any measurement takes place at a point in time. When you take the measurement again it is at a second point in time. Because the pace of change is accelerating, the interval between time 1 and time 2 is getting shorter.

Follow this to a logical conclusion and you realize – at least in the business world –the intervals are getting so short that measurement is moving from periodic to continual. A company's financial books used to be closed annually, then quarterly, now the norm is monthly. However, in 1999 Cisco Systems could close their worldwide financial books daily and in 2000 could do so at one hour's notice.

Notice how a trend or direction unfolds in many of the examples I have given, until at some point the logic guiding it flips. When measurement is continual, for example, accounting is no longer a historical ledger and it becomes an operating tool. Cisco can respond to threats and opportunities in real time, thereby causing outcomes rather than reacting to them.

What else happens when you shift from periodic to continual? This is a good topic for thinking about when I'm lap swimming, on the treadmill, or in the shower. For example, most businesses bring out new product or service models periodically. The car industry has been built around annual model changes. With so much of the value of today's cars locked in its software and electronic connections, why not download upgrades as they occur instead of waiting for the annual model change? Imagine, you and your car go to sleep at night and, while you dream, your car gets smarter through downloads. There is enough difference here to rattle the basic business model.

In times of rapid change, oxymorons are not. Therefore, find a paradox and look for resolution in larger contexts. Here is how it works: think of a pair of opposites in business, define their simultaneity or a larger concept that embraces both, then look for examples that already exist. A typical business example is price and quality.

Conventional wisdom says that the better the quality the higher the price. However, unlike most other businesses, computers operate with increasing returns economics where the better it is the cheaper it gets. The more intrinsic the computer to business, the more the paradox spreads. Ask yourself: when my company improves the quality of its offer, does it tend to raise or lower its price accordingly? It is a great indicator of new versus old mindset, of past versus future orientation. Flexibility and order are another couplet to try this on.

Coining "mass customizing" was probably my most successful discovery using this method (see pp. 115–22). The creative idea came to me through such an exercise. I had written "mass" and "customized" in a column of opposites. Because I had only a vague notion of what the couplet meant, I wrote a definition of these paired opposites expressed simultaneously: the mass-production, distribution, and delivery of customized goods and services. Then I started looking around for early or meta-examples. As they piled up and various technologies showed they could facilitate mass customizing in very different ways, the concept took off, first in my mind, then in *Future Perfect*, and now throughout the business world.

I am very fortunate that my field changes so rapidly. So much is so new that there are abundant opportunities for creative ideas. I will leave you with an idea I am working on now.

There are basic recurrent patterns in the natural world: spirals and helixes, spheres and explosions, packing and cracking, meanders and ripples, branching and fractals. Will these patterns also operate in an economy rooted in the science of biology, that is in the future bio-economy? Let us take one pattern and see.

Biology works at tiny, small, medium, and large levels – that is DNA, organisms, species, and ecology – and nature works from the bottom up (see pp. 179–83). Current investment is virtually all in the molecular but, as the bio-economy scales up, there is a good chance that it may do so fractally, that molecular approaches and designs will appear recursively, in larger forms at product, company, industry, and economy levels. If so, will this happen simultaneously or in successive waves of development?

As the bio-economy unfolds, economic value will be created from very small things. Then, just as DNA shapes organisms, molecular value will shape enterprise. Further along, new species of enterprise will evolve. Do we have to wait many decades for the bio-economy to mature before molecular value will manifest itself in ecology and environment? Are ecological economics possible or only as metaphor and political movements?

Finally, as you think about the computational platform for the bio-economy, ponder this. Fractals are largely spatial phenomena. Why not think of them as operating in all dimensions: space, time, and mass. When you do,

> Fractal time is *déjà vu*,
> fractal space is point of view, and
> fractal mass is evolu.

It is terrible as poetry, but as a mnemonic ditty it meets my two most important criteria for coming up with new ideas: keep it playful and powerful. If it is playful without being powerful, it is entertaining but trite. If it is powerful without being playful, it is important but boring. Go for that simultaneity. That is my intention for this book.

# Part II

Economy

# I

# Future perfect

Time, space, and mass are the basic dimensions of the universe and the economy and your business are part of the universe, so they have got to be the basic dimensions of these too. This was the touchstone that stated me on 15 years (so far) of my most productive thinking. Here, I trace how the basics of the universe get expressed in science, translated into technologies, then find their ways into business and, ultimately, into how we manage our businesses. *Lesson from the Future:* unless the basic dimensions of the universe change, these will remain the touchstones, what you can always come back to in order to understand – perhaps before others – what lies ahead.

Since *Future Perfect* was first published a decade ago, many of the ideas I introduced in the original edition have become intrinsic to business.

Competing on the basis of speed, for example, is now assumed to be part of any business strategy; ten years ago the idea was just being born. "Any Time" and "Any Place", the titles of the first two chapters, were just quirky phrases back then.

Similarly, mass customizing, a term coined in *Future Perfect*, has since entered into general currency.

The framework that I created ten years ago explains these developments and holds promise for many more breakthroughs in the future. It is based on a simple syllogism. The dimensions of the known universe. The minor premise is a case in point – that your business is part of the universe. Juxtaposing the two premises, the conclusion is that time, space, and mass are fundamental dimensions of your business. *Future Perfect* is an exploration of the power that comes from embracing this conclusion.

In *Future Perfect*, I treat time in terms of the consumers' perspective and the providers' point of view. The consumers' sense of time is that they want their products and services any time, whereas the providers have focused more on being able to operate in real time. These two notions are now very familiar, but it is how companies deal with lag time – that is, the gap between identifying a needed action and actually taking it – that will make the most important mark on time in the decade to come.

Historically, when a company does not own connecting links in a value chain, then relations with other corporations above and below it on the chain have been at arm's length. Purchasing raw materials and intermediate goods from suppliers, shipping finished goods to distributors, and getting them to the final consumers was a lengthy process. From beginning to end, from raw materials to consumption, many value chains were often more than one year long. Eliminating lag times such as these will be a major focus in every part of business in the decade ahead.

Time has become intrinsic to business logic during the past decade and, since this has happened, the start-to-finish time-lapse of value chains has begun to shrink. How quickly a business can move from concept to customer – that is, from an idea, through its development, and into a product or service that is bought and used by customers – has become a basic yardstick of success. Inventory churn and cash flow are early, related measures. Today, every activity may be measured and the time it takes to do it shrunk. Why type a note, print it, put it in an envelope, "snail mail" it through the post office, and so on? Indeed, why even print and then fax it? Today, by e-mail, we just click on "send." Why build physical prototypes of new airplane and automobile models when computer simulations give more accurate answers in a fraction of the time? Boeing builds more than 90 percent of a new plane this way, while Ford builds less than 10 percent of a new car using such analytical prototypes. Ford moved from less than 10 percent to about 90 percent within four years. Competing on the basis of how fast you develop and implement anything is to be measured in multiples (300 percent, five times as fast), not marginals (3 percent, a one-fifth improvement).

Executives who used to worry about the time value of money now manage the money value of time. Strange things happen in the economy and in corporations when time and money fuse. In pre-industrial times, payment for goods and letters of credit might have had to wait months for ships to arrive. Industrial economies cut the lag time from months and weeks to days and hours. Clearing and communicating financial transactions in today's information economy take a fraction of a second.

Similarly, gross national product is the stockpile of money. As Chris Meyer of Ernst & Young pointed out, when you introduce the dimension of time, it becomes the stockpile of money times the velocity of money. If the velocity of money is infinite, then you do not need any money (or, say, only one dollar). While this, of course, is *reductio ad absurdum*, it does point out the implications of speeding up the time it takes to move money and other financial instruments through the world's economies. Regulatory restraints are in disarray, convertibility restraints (the fungibility of money) scarcely exist in the electronic age, and the information infrastructure is moving in ever closer to that infinite velocity.

Work and personal time are also fused. Computers, faxes, cellular phones, beepers, and e-mail were supposed to save you time. Yet, people find themselves working longer, rather than less. The focus on time seems only to give people less time. Can we expect a reaction and focus to develop in which people seek to expand time, not shrink it? How might this happen? Well, time is measured horizontally, so if we thought of measuring it vertically, perhaps we could find some more of it.

Vertical time, according to Vivian Wright of Hewlett-Packard, means that, in a given moment, you have all the time you need. To grasp this you need not be a Zen master. Just think about how time flies when you are having a wonderful go at something. Expressing this in corollary fashion, you packed an enormity into that seemingly fleeting moment. Westerners are experts at zooming along ever faster in horizontal time, but novices at dropping into the fold of vertical time. As computer technologies become less frustrating and more engaging to consumers, perhaps we will drop in longer and more often.

Space, along with time, has also become a major shaper of businesses, industries, and the economy during the last decade. The changes brought about by the evolving infrastructure, for example, will reshape and, hence, respace how business is conducted in all industries. Much of this respacing is happening in actual physical space, as in neighborhood clinics, distance classrooms, and automatic teller machine branches. The most radical respacing in the past decade, however, emerged quite unexpectedly. Paradoxically, it involves non-physical space, that is a space created by information technologies and that resides only in the perception and mind of the viewer: cyberspace.

First coined by the fiction writer William Gibson, cyberspace is that place you "are" when you are really tuned-in to your favorite music, to an important phone conversation or to an engaging dialogue on the Internet – in other words, when you are connected via information technology. It exists at all the nodes and crossroads where your non-physical presence hooks up with digital information. According to Kevin Kelly, executive editor or *Wired* magazine, it is "that territory where the counterintuitive logic of distributed networks meets the odd behavior of human society."[1] Cyberspace is the electronic ether. The paradox is that you are simultaneously disembodied and superconnected. Cyberspace is as much about mass as it is about space or, rather, it is about non-space and no-matter. An intriguing quality of cyberspace is that, unlike traditional resources that are finite and get used up, the more we use it, the more we have. It operates with different set of economics.

Cyberspace, we have come to say, is a "virtual" reality. It captures the essential nature of something minus its material existence. Virtual products and services are the no-matter of the late 1990s. Flight simulators for pilot training, for example, are such highly developed virtual realities that pilots often comment they are even better than the real thing. Virtual malls are the retailers' dream of electronic commerce, although not something significant on the near horizon. The desire for virtual businesses spawns talk about virtual organizations to run them. At the very least, this is a desire to run businesses with no overheads and only minimal costs. In the extreme it is a wish for organizations and all their problems to just go away, an even more distant dream than is electronic commerce.

Virtual offerings were not yet on the radar screen when the original edition of *Future Perfect* came out. Software and services were the chief manifestations of no-matter that I dealt with in the original edition. In the intervening years, information has become the most important form of no-matter. Before that we spoke mainly of data and, in the future, we will pay increasing attention to knowledge.

Data are the basic building blocks, namely numbers, words, sounds, and images. Information is the arrangement of data into meaningful patterns, first separately and, recently, mixed together in multimedia. Knowledge, the application and productive use of information, ratchets no-matter's value even higher. Sounds can be thought of as notes (data), for example, and when arranged in a musical system, they become information. Depending upon the skill of the composer and performer, the results can be greater knowledge. A monthly credit card bill has a number of data points that are arranged to give you information. If they are arranged by spending categories (travel, entertainment, and by whether or not the items are deductible), they might help you know how to manage expenses better.

The core technology of every economy becomes the foundation for economic growth. These were industrial technologies in the previous era and, therefore, all business industrialized. Even agriculture mechanized, resulting in the transformation from family farming to large-scale agribusiness. The core of today's economy is information technology and, therefore, all businesses "informationalize," a phenomenon I wrote about in *2020 Vision* (see pp. xxx–xxx).

Informationalized business means the economic value that comes from creating, processing, communicating, and selling information grows significantly faster than the value added by traditional goods and services.

While the value of the traditional core product or service itself shrinks, the information content of that offering grows proportionately ever larger. Indeed, the informationalized businesses often become worth more than the parents from which they sprang in the first place. That is why American Airlines makes more money from its SABRE reservations systems than by flying people around on airplanes, why Ford makes more money financing cars than making and selling them, and why Marriott makes more money from management contracts to run hotels than from owning the brick and mortar and real-estate. No-matter matters.

Simply put, smart products and services are better than dumb ones and knowledge-based offerings represent the next generation of no-matter. They are an important step beyond information-based growth. Knowledge is information that is applied to something and, as such, it is a process. Knowledge, unlike information, evolves. Knowledge is alive, information is not. By the year 2006, knowledge-based business will be as different from information-based business as the latter are today from mere databases. At the present, however, we see only a slight shift and we are just beginning to appreciate the distinction.

Knowledge-based offerings can anticipate what you want and search and find it for you. An Otis elevator will know when it is about to break down and calls its own repair person. If you once ordered hypoallergenic pillows in a hotel, then similar pillows should be in your room each time you check-in to a hotel of that chain anywhere in the world. The pillows are data points in your information profile; getting those pillows into your room minutes before you arrive is the productive action that elevates it to a knowledge-based service. Imagine Psychic pizza delivered to your door 15 minutes before you knew you would want it or your money back!

Knowledge-based offering update instantaneously and adjust to changing circumstances. Non-linear dynamics and chaos theory are playing an important role here in adjusting things as diverse as airplane wings, earthquake-resistant buildings, and heart monitors. A thermos keeps hot coffee hot and iced tea cold. How does it know? Products and services will increasingly be expected to know and to adjust automatically. They will also be able to filter information and then make and act on recommendations.

All products and services can be ratcheted up in value to be knowledge based. For each of the characteristics I have mentioned, ask yourself if your products and services do that and, if not, find out what it would take for them to do so, because this is the direction in which you will have to move. The provider must ask, what is the knowledge value in a pair of socks, in a home mortgage, in a kitchen sink, or in room services?

The more you use knowledge-based offerings, the smarter both you and they get. If the offerings are linked back to those who make or create them, then these upstream players also get smarter. More and more products and services will be expected to have memory, hence they will learn with usage. Early generations will have to be trained, as with the young family of personal digital assistants; later generations will have learned (future perfect tense) by themselves, without the need for complicated programming.

Knowledge-based offerings also have relatively short life cycles. Each constantly adjusting and ever smarter version is like one frame in a motion picture reel. Each frame is a customized version. They come so continuously that the flow becomes more important than the frame, which is only a tangible expression of a product in a frozen drop of time. Knowledge materialized from the no-matter flows into the product. If the flow is the constant and more important way to look at the true offering, then you are treating products as though they are services. Since, in the industrial era, we treated services as though they were products, it is appropriate in this information era to come full circle and reverse the treatment. Knowledge-based products will behave and perform like services.

Since knowledge-based offerings have highly specific targeting and customize themselves to particular criteria, they bring us to mass customizing. Mass customizing is an oxymoron, the putting together of seemingly contradictory notions, like jumbo shrimp and artificial intelligence. Or, as my then-teenage son told me a few years ago, "Oh, like a parent's joke."

If you want to understand and be able to use the power of mass customizing, then you must appreciate the logic behind the concept. This paradoxical logic, the simultaneity of opposites, did not originate in business, of course. The religious notion of the trinity, the governmental notion of balance of power, and the psychological notion of ambivalence are variations of this same logic: to allow for the coexistence of opposites, to embrace contradiction as an indication of a larger truth. The key is to embrace and transcend the paradox, rather than be limited by it.

Unlike other domains, however, the applications of the paradox to economic life require technologies that can handle contradictions. Pre-industrial technologies were not suited to this task because they were premised on small volumes with high unit costs. Industrial technologies were premised on the opposite approach: high volumes and low unit costs. Business had to wait for today's technologies to merge the two into mass customization, the production and distribution of customized goods and services on a mass basis.

Mass customizing is related to the Japanese-led concept of continuous improvement. Continuous improvement is simply an intermediate step between mass production and mass customization. The mass-production model of the industrial economy held that you could have either low-cost, standardized goods and services or high-quality, customized ones, but not both simultaneously. Since then, continuous improvement has demonstrated that you can have low cost and high-quality simultaneously, while mass customizing has demonstrated that you can simultaneously mass produce, distribute, and deliver customized goods and services.

Mass customizing is not restricted to products and services. It also applied to customers and markets. Where a mass customized product is a one-of-a-kind manufacture on a large scale, the masscustomized market takes products of standardized manufacture and locates the one particular item that is customized to the individual's needs. The goods may be mass produced, while the customizing occurs in the speedy matching-up process. There are two important questions to ask yourself. What elements in the product-market mix do you want to mass customize? And where along the value chain do you want to mass customize – in design, manufacture, sale, service? Be selective. A good rule of thumb is to mass customize as much as necessary and as little as possible.

Our knowledge about mass customizing technologies appeared about 15 years ago and is already mature. Our ability to mass customize our businesses is in its growth phase now. Remember that business is what you do and organization is how you do it. Mass customizing of organizations is still in its gestation, not yet instantaneous, costless, seamless, or frictionless. These are great goals for teams and organizations, but we are nowhere near this kind of maturity in our managerial or organizational skills. Groupware tools, like Lotus Notes, are simply first-quarter yearnings.

Why have we embraced these new precepts for our businesses, but not yet for the organizations that run them? It is time to re-examine some basic notions about how we organize our economic activities.

There are many precepts that the business world accepts as given, fixed, and true. Business accepts it as axiomatic, for example, that to survive it must change as fast as the environment it operates in changes. Otherwise, it will fall behind and eventually fail. Business also takes it as axiomatic that you manage and organize according to the business you are in. When the business changes, you must change your management and organization, otherwise a gap will develop and grow. Taken together, the arrival of environmental changes causes business to change and this in turn causes organization change. What seems so boringly obvious at first blush, however, is exactly what gets us into trouble when we follow these precepts blindly. Each of these two percepts by itself is true – it is the combination of the two that is lethal.

The external environment – technology, economy, society, and so on – is changing so fast that business must scurry to keep us. Organizations, however, simply cannot run that fast. So our organizations do not change as fast as do the businesses that they are managing. The gap between real-time businesses and their not-so-real-time organizations seems as permanent and growing as the national deficit.

Management consultants, academics, journalists, and gurus make brilliant careers and handsome livings off this gap. Ironically, organization change itself has become a big business. Consultants, for example, will sell you an organization-change study or process. For a lot of money, time, and energy, you and they will focus on closing the gap. It is a fool's errand.

Implementing the necessary organization change will take you, say, two years. If you start in 2001, by the time you complete the change you will have an organization perfectly appropriate for 2001. But by then you have a 2003 business run with a 2001 organization. By the time you get there, there is not there any more and you still have problems with your organization. Time to hire another round of organization change consultants?

Wrong. It is time to change the precept. Rather than coming from a model that works to get the organization to catch up, we would be much better off if we accepted that – using this model – the organization can never catch up. Instead, try using models that never fall behind in the first place.

That is a neat trick, you might say. How can I pull that off?

By confronting the fact that business operates by economic rules of the marketplace, whereas organizations operate by the social, psychological, and political rules of the workplace. If we want businesses and their organizations to work together in lock step, rather than in lag step, then they must operate by the same rules. This is the simple essence of the new model of management and organizations that will grow during the next decade: organizations run by marketplace economics, rather than by rules of power and status

Today, to take one of the examples from the original edition of the book, business is as interested in getting entrepreneurship into large corporations as it was a decade ago. But it still has not learned that entrepreneurs play a money game, while mangers play a power and status game. It still confuses economic reality with psychic mentality.

When an employee's promotion comes with a larger office and carpeting, it is invariably accepted as a reward of office, conferring the appropriate increase in power and status. When employees traveling for the company are allowed to stay at a Ritz Carlton or Four Seasons hotel, they never turn that down in favor of a Quality Inn or Holiday Inn. Few would be given the choice of taking the financial difference involved and investing it instead in the business, in product development, or more sales coverage. Any why should they, unless both business and organization operate by the same logic and scorecard.

Reviewing what I wrote a decade ago, it seems clear that since then the corporate world has embraced the business implications of *Future Perfect* and that the organization precepts are yet to come. They are still correct, but they just have not happened yet. In the original edition I argued that this is because there is a basic progression from changes in the universe to changes in science, then technology, then business, and, last, in organization. We are finally at the end of the progression. In the decade ahead we will see many new ways of organizing. Organizations that run in real time – like the business they represent – transcend space, run on no-matter, and mass customize.

I would like to end here with a personal observation. I closed the original book, *Future Perfect*, with a story about my meeting "a very unique executive." Little did I know then that years later this gentleman would turn out to be the biggest swindler in the history of modern banking. He was, indeed, very unique.

Although I did not name him then, he was Agha Hasan Abedi and at the time he was the head of the Bank of Credit & Commerce International. When I met him, BCCI was esteemed by all the world's economic and political leaders. Years later, in 1991, the bank crashed and the most massive bank fraud in history came to light. Heading the list of those duped, for example, was a $2 billion loss from the personal fortune of the ruler of Abu Dhabi. Thousands of ordinary people around the world lost their lives' savings.

London's *Financial Times* called him "a man of breathtaking audacity and cunning" and, in Abedi's 1995 obituary, the *Wall Street Journal* called him a global criminal "cheerfully going about the business of pillaging the world's financial systems." You can imagine my horror when the *Financial Times* (11 November 1991) published a letter Abedi had written, in which he explained his philosophy to the son of the bank's chief executive, by referencing "the article of Professor Stanley M. Davis."

The Bank of Credit & Commerce International episode made me think that powerful ideas have power that can be used for both good and bad. Peripheral visionaries see a long way into the future, but a bit off to the side. Despite this bizarre and cautionary exception, it is a pleasure to see *Future Perfect*'s ideas of any time, any place, no-matter, and mass customizing take such firm roots and bear such fruitful results in the world economy.

# 2

Crunching: the first
half of the information
economy

This excerpt establishes the basic footprint of architecture of
the information economy: four forms × four functions. They
are still the touchstone, the foundation upon which to build.
The fundamental forms are numbers, words, sounds, and
images; the basic functions of information are creating, processing, transmitting, and storing it. These have not changed.
Storing information has become a relatively minor activity, while
portals – the entry point or locating function – is comparatively
new and major, but that belongs to the second half of the information economy. *Lesson from the Future*: as virtually infinite
bandwidth, at nominal cost, becomes commonplace, sound and
image will become as basic to daily business activity as numbers
and words are. This has yet to happen, but it will.

The first time it happens is often in the shower. You catch a glimpse of yourself in the bathroom mirror and unwillingly note the trespass of time. Somewhere in mid-life, instead of thinking how old you are, you begin to wonder how many years you have left.

Wherever and whenever this happens, usually and meaningfully we change the way we lead our lives. If we are exquisitely aware that our lives are finite, we are often more tolerant of the little things and focus on what is most important to us. Economies also reach a mid-point in their lives and a clear awareness of our economy's life cycle can have a similarly transforming effect.

Everyone is aware that we are now in what is generally known as an information economy. But the phrase is used so glibly and super-ficially that is has become almost meaningless. While the information economy began in the mid-1950s, most of us were not even aware of it until the 1970s. For two decades nobody knew we had switched economies. Then, for one more decade a few intellec-tuals and business visionaries knew and acted, while almost everyone else merely discussed and debated. By the 1980s, there was general agreement that we were in a fundamentally different economy. Still, we debated and discussed and missed opportunities to act on the basis of our insight.

We are now offered a new insight and another opportunity. This current economy will come to an end in the 2020s, about seven decades after it began. We are already halfway through it. Fortysomething and halfway through!

What does this mean? What can we do with this insight? Should we be depressed or energized? Mid-life realizations about both our-selves and our economy are risky opportunities. If we take advantage of these opportunities, they can be transforming. If we shrug them off, we are unlikely to secure the gains that will make the difference in our personal and collective lives.

With our information economy at mid-life and recession an ever present concern, the essentials of every business are being altered so fundamentally that you had better not be in the same business five to ten years from now that you are in today. You had better be the first not the last to know why and the first to know what to do about it. If after that short time you are still in the same business, it is likely that you will also be on your way out of business altogether. What is worse, you will not find out until it is too late. Marginal improvements will not be enough to stay competitive. You can get 5, 10, 15 percent improvements in what you are doing by doing the same thing, only a bit better. But your competition will go for improvements in multiples. To attain 100, 300, 500 percent improvements, you cannot do the same thing better. You have to do something fundamentally different and, in the process, your business will be fundamentally transformed.

Today, *information-based enhancements have become the main avenue for revitalizing mature businesses and transforming them into new ones.*

In every economy, the core technology becomes the basis for revitalization and growth. Information technologies are the core for today's economy and to survive all businesses must *informationalize*. From small mom-and-pop stores to giant global corporations, the point to grasp is not merely that all economic activities will depend upon information to create and control their destiny. We have heard that already. And while it is true, this truth manifests itself so slowly – over decades – that people have tired of it. For many, it is unpoured honey.

Instead of focusing on its not-so-newness, we must focus on the growing power and consequences of this truth. The point is that the economic value from generating, using, and selling information is growing significantly faster than the value added by producing traditional goods and services. Mature businesses will continue, just as do agriculture and industry, but they represent a shrinking proportion of the total economy and require an ever smaller proportion of the economy to meet their resource needs. Increasing the information content of any product of service, to make a smart version of a not-so-smart one, will demand more resource inputs and will yield more productive outputs. All businesses will get increasingly smart in this sense or yield to more informationalized competitors.

The value of any product can be increased by incorporating intelligence, information content, and services. Businesses can modernize even their most mature products and services by embedding information features and functions. Increased value does not come from material changes so much as from new intangibles. Choice, variety, and service embedded in traditional products create smart products and new market opportunities.

Profitability from the new features, in fact, often exceeds the profit from the original product or service. The more information you put into a product or the more you are able to use a product to pull out information, the more you evolve beyond the original purpose into new ones. These new ones, which are based on information, may present even far greater opportunities than the original.

## A quick lesson in mastering the architecture of information

It is useful to look at information in terms of its forms and functions. Here, form is simply the shape and structure of information and function refers to the actions or activities performed in its regard. Most information in our economy can be classified into four different forms and four distinct functions (see Figure 2.1). These terms are rather self-evident and it is very difficult to say much about one without drifting into a discussion of the other. Their power comes from understanding their interplay.

In our economy information comes in four forms: data, text, sound, and image. These forms are all mental impressions that we receive through the senses and, in this economy, the senses of sight and hearing are the most important.

Other forms that information comes in relate to other senses. Taste, touch, and smell, for example, may become important in the bio-economy of the future, but their commercial engineering is many decades away. Other senses, such as intuition and extrasensory perception, are also in their infancy insofar as commercial applications are involved and they too belong to the next economy, if at all. Neural network computers and artificial intelligence will

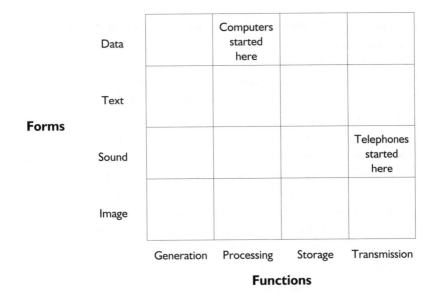

**Figure 2.1** The architecture of information.

have to evolve much further before we may even understand the potentials of these senses.

Data are any or all the facts, numbers, letters, symbols, and the like that can be processed or produced by a computer. Data existed before computers, of course, but it is the computer's unique ability to handle data that led to the information economy itself. When text, sound, and image are reduced to the raw bits of "0s" and "1s" in a computer, they are data. Data, however, most commonly refers to numbers.

Text is written language, to distinguish it from spoken language, which technology treats simply as one form of sound.

Sound is what we hear and, in this economy, we hear basically the sound of voice and music. Radio, telephone, records, tape recorders, and computers are the kinds of products we use to handle this form of information and for decades they were very different businesses. The products and their functions, competition, and government regulations were different and did not compete with one another. In today's economy, that is no longer true.

Images are visual forms. They can be photographs or drawings. They can be artistic or practical, realistic or interpretive. They can be presentations or representations, impressions or expressions – as long as they can be seen. Charts and diagrams, faces and landscapes are all images. Some are in black and white, some in colors. The scanned image of a page of text and data is treated as a single image, although new programs have learned to transform them once again. Thus, the copier, fax, printer, and scanner are four separate machines performing essentially similar functions and, therefore, are likely to continue merging in the future. In the information economy, however, there are some basic distinctions between still images and moving ones and between natural images and graphically created ones.

These basic forms of information start to get more complex when you realize what can be done with them – their function. Basically, we do four things with information: generate it, process it, store it, and transmit it. Anything that is done with any product or service that deals with any of the four forms of information can be described in this way. Doing one or more of these is what will make the information aspect of business become the most valuable part in the future.

Generation, the first function, takes information that exists in the environment and captures it for presentation in one of the four forms. An abacus captures the numbers of an accountant and generates a ledger, a typewriter captures the words of an author and generates a book, a recording device captures the sound of a guitar and generates a record or tape, and a photograph captures the image of a landscape and generates a picture.

Generating information in this economy does not refer to the creative spark of intellect, but to preparing information to be sent in a form that is easily understood by the receiver. Essentially, this means digitizing it, arranging it into "bits," the basic unit of information with which a computer works.

Processing, the second function, is where the computer made its first great contribution, starting with data processing, then word processing, and, currently, voice and image processing, thus covering all forms. The processing function of the computer converts, edits, analyzes, computes, and synthesizes. By the use of semiconductor technology, information is manipulated and transformed. Although today's computers combine generation, processing, and storage, the steps are as distinct as capturing an image on film, developing, enhancing, and enlarging it, then finding a place to keep the information contained in that photograph in intangible form. In the programs they create, software firms generate the rules by which gathered information will be processed.

Storage, the third function, takes information in one of the four forms and keeps it for later use. In the time of the Pharaohs, text and data were stored on tablets and the Lascaux cave drawings stored images tens of thousands of years before that. Only sound had to wait for the industrial era to be stored on records, tapes, and discs.

Transmission, the fourth information function, comes to us courtesy of the telephone. Simply put, it is the sending and receiving of all forms of information from one point to another at the speed of electromagnetic waves on coaxial cables and at the speed of light on fiber optic cables. Whereas storage transfers information across time, transmission moves it across space. It is the distribution function and includes many activities such as broadcasting, switching, networking, reception, signal processing, collection, and display. While computers dominated the first three functions – generation, processing, and storage – telecommunications has excelled in the fourth function, transmission. More specifically, computers began in the data processing cell and telecommunications began in the sound transmission cell of the information infrastructure.

All the combinations and configurations on the form/function grid produce an endless variety of information-based tools, products, services, and businesses. At a simple product level, for example, attach a tape recorder to a telephone receiver and it stores the sound transmissions. Now we are using three functions and one form. Upgrade to a voice mail system and we can also process the information: listen to messages in any desired order rather than having to listen to them in the order they arrived, send one message to many people, ask to be transferred for further assistance, etc. Four functions, one form. Integrate the capacity to send documents and even graphic designs along with the voice message and we are covering all forms and functions. Traditional computing separates form and function in the way software is designed, but new approaches (with the unfortunate name of "object orientation") combine them and make them easier to work with in unison. Combining more forms and more functions equals more added value and more business.

We can go to sound stores now in many cities and "download" any random arrangement of songs we want onto a tape, customized to our own tastes, at little additional cost. Replace the tape with a disc and we upgrade yet again. A disc recorder combines musical sound processing with generation and storage, so that the order of songs, for example, can be moved about. We can also record our own voice onto the sound track of any songs we choose. High tech at low price is creating a whole new market in sound processing and storage, as well as professional quality music recordings that can be produced at home. Developments like these are actually taking place in each portion of the form/function grid.

This simple information grid provides entrepreneurs and managers with a roadmap to the second half of the information economy. Not only can all products and services that deal with information be understood in these terms, but also all companies can use this grid to build their future businesses on the evolving economic infrastructure. It can be used in three ways. At its simplest, any and all information can be understood in terms of this one conceptual map. Second, if you are confused by all the information vendors and what they have available or even if you yourself are an information vendor and not confused, it will help you to organize your own information infrastructure and what you might do with it. Third, whatever business you are in, it will become driven by information during the next several decades. So, the better your grasp of information's forms and functions and the more of them you use, the greater your advantage.

# 3

## Connecting: the second half of the information economy

In practical terms, time, space, and mass translate into speed, connectivity, and intangibles and become the basic drivers of the information economy. Every aspect of business and organization will have to operate and change in real time. Everything is becoming electronically connected to everything else: products, people, companies, countries, everything. This will continue and accelerate. Every offer (product or service) has both tangible and intangible economic value and the intangibles are growing the faster of the two. *Lesson from the Future*: for at least this next decade, speed, connectivity, and intangibles will continue to be the most important forces around which to build businesses and the economy.

Has the pace of change accelerated way beyond your comfort zone? Are the rule that guided your decisions in the past no longer reliable? If so, you are just like everyone else who is paying attention. You are not imagining things.

The elements of changes that are driving these momentous shifts are based on the fundamental dimensions of the universe itself: time, space, and mass. Since the economy and your business are part of the universe, time, space, and mass are the fundamental dimensions of them as well. Until recently this notion was too abstract to be very useful. Now, we are realizing the extraordinary power this insight has for the business world.

Almost instantaneous communication and computation, for example, are shrinking time and focusing us on speed. Connectivity is putting everybody and everything on-line in one way or another and has led to "the death of distance,"[1] a shrinking of space. Intangible value of all kinds, like service and information, is growing explosively, reducing the importance of tangible mass.

Connectivity, speed, and intangibles – the derivatives of time, space, and mass – are blurring the rules and redefining our businesses and our lives. They are destroying solutions, such as mass-production, segmented pricing, and standardized jobs, that worked for the relatively slow, unconnected industrial world. The fact is, something enormous is happening all around you, enough to make you feel as if you are losing your balance and seeing double. So relax. You are experiencing things as they really are, a BLUR. Ignore these forces and BLUR will make you miserable and your business hopeless. Harness and leverage them and you can enter the world of BLUR, move to its cadence, and once again see the world clearly.

What will you see? A meltdown of all traditional boundaries. In the BLUR world, products and services are merging. Buyers sell and sellers buy. Neat value chains are messy economic webs. Homes are offices. No longer is there a clear line between structure and process, owning and using, knowing and learning, real and virtual. Less and less separates employee and employer. In the world of capital – itself as much a liability as an asset – value moves so fast you cannot tell stock from flow. On every front, opposites are blurring.

We offer a lens through which you can see BLUR for a moment of static clarity, much as strobe-lit people seem to freeze in poses on a dance floor. Don't think you'll ever slow down BLUR, let alone bring it to a halt. Its constant acceleration is here to stay and those who miss that point will miss everything. Your job as a manager, as an entrepreneur, as a consumer, and as an individual is to master the BLUR, to keep the acceleration going, to keep your world changing and off balance. Stop trying to slow it down. Stop trying to clarity it, codify it, explain it. Recognize it. Learn its new rules. You will then be able to move at BLUR's speed – and discover that you can thrive in amazing new ways.

You are ready to join the dance on the other side of the strobes, where you will move at the speed of BLUR. Remember, the frozen image is false. The reality is continual motion, a BLUR strorm.

## Connectivity, speed, and intangibles: the trinity of the BLUR

We may tell ourselves that connectivity, speed, and intangibles hold no surprises, but each has gone through its own metamorphosis in recent times.

On the evening of 17 January 1991, Chris was flying home from Los Angeles to Boston when the pilot announced that Operation Desert Storm had begun. He then broadcast the audio portion of CNN's report over the DC-10's entertainment system so that the passengers could listen to a description by a reporter in Baghdad, relayed through Israel, transmitted worldwide, picked up by the airplane, and sent to their earphones. Given the importance of the event, what would you do? Within moments, Chris called his wife, Mary, in Boston to tell her the news. This all happened through an airborne-connected network that was far more powerful than anything that military pilots had in the Korean War, just 40 years earlier. How was this possible? By connecting everything to everything, in real time.

In rapid succession the deregulation of telecommunications, the

miniaturization of satellites, and the development of mobile technologies have made connection available to anyone, anytime, anyplace.
Now, with the explosive take-off of the Internet, we have entered the
second half of the information economy, which uses the computer
less for data crunching and more for connecting: people to people,
machine to machine, product to service, network to network, organization to organization, and all the combinations thereof.

In 1999, low earth-orbiting satellites will bring these capabilities
everywhere on the planet. By the year 200 telecommunication networks in the USA will carry more electronic data than voice. More
astonishing, voice will be less than 2 percent of the traffic by 2003.
Think of telephones running on the Internet, rather than the
Internet running on the telephone system! The cost of global telecommunications will fall drastically, just as long-distance costs have
done over the past 20 years. This massive increase in connection
will change the way all business is conducted, turn current business
and economic models on their heads, and take us ever deeper and
faster into BLUR.

Mobile telephones, pagers, voice mail systems, bar code scan-
ners, satellite telephones, e-mail, global positioning satellites, and all
the rest of the electronic gizmos that will connect us are just the vis-
ible part of the connectivity story. Once these things connect with
each other, their actions will trigger domino effects and change the
way the economy behaves.

The stock market crash of October 1987 was caused by computerized trades, none of which were linked explicitly. The damage was
done by the interaction of independent investor instructions – a kind
of connected network of trading programs. Similarly, the 1965
Northeast power blackout was the worst in history because of the
connections shared by the utilities in the power grid. These connections translated an overload at one point in the system into a
cascading failure throughout the grid. That is why the trading limits
installed after the 1987 financial debacle are called "circuit breakers."

These examples illustrate the importance of connection: a single
automatic circuit breaker, a cruncher, has limited impact. Connect
1000 of them and there is no telling how the system will behave.

The first use of the financial circuit breaker, in October 1997, was in response to frenzied selling in markets in Asia earlier in the day, further evidence of the connectedness of the global system.

The instant communication of the Gulf War is an amazing story about connectivity, but a trivial one about speed. News has always traveled fast. When we speak of speed, we are talking about how the sheer velocity of business has increased over the last decade. Take, for example, the dramatic drop in the time between sending and receiving. Order a laptop from PC Connection at 2:00 a.m., receive it custom configured at home 10 hours later. Similarly, the time-lapse is evaporating between producing and selling and pur-chasing and delivering. In Tokyo, you can order your customized Toyota on Monday and be driving it on Friday.

Speed is the foreshortening of product life cycles from years to months or even weeks and speed is the worldwide electronic net-work over which financial institutions transfer money at the rate of $41 billion a minute. For the individual, speed is scores of messages a day, creating near continuous communication. Miss a day and your world moves on without you. Accelerated product life cycles and time-based competition have become part of the business lingo. These experiences change people's perceptions. We now expect real-time responsiveness, 24 hours of every day of the year. This premium placed on anytime, real-time responsiveness is just one example of the growing importance of intangible value.

The intangible portion of the economy has grown quietly, alter-ing how we see the world without calling too much attention of itself. It takes four forms. *Services*, which have dominated the econ-omy for decades, are the most familiar. They include everything from hamburger flippers to brain surgeons. The second is *informa-tion*, such as the specialized knowledge in databases, the content of George Lucas's Star Wars empire, and the shadows cast by activi-ties and transactions onto credit card bills and stock tickers. The third is the *service component of products*. Computer simulation ser-vices, on everything from automobiles and architecture to windows and wallpaper, commonly allow customers to try out different con-figurations before ordering the actual product. Fourth are *emotions*, the trust and loyalty that people feel for a brand, the prestige conveyed by a label, the attraction exerted by a celebrity on the stage, screen, or playing field.

DreamWorks SKG is a powerful expression of the value of intangibles. Formed with a mere $250 million, it was mobbed by eager investors who drove the market capitalization to $2 billion when the company, which had no studio and nothing in production, went public. The attraction was the intangible value of its founders, Steven Spielberg, Jeffrey Katzenberg, and David Greffen, each of whom is a star in the entertainment business even though their faces are never on the screen. Intangibles are at work in the form of innovation, brands, trust, and relationships.

Intangible value is growing much faster than the tangible. However, in the connected economy, the increasing demand for intangibles also brings with it some new economic wrinkles. Compare succotash and software. With succotash, two pounds cost twice as much as one pound. But with software the second copy is pretty much free. Further, if we cook one pound of succotash, we eat it or you do. Software, however, can be duplicated again and again with no additional cost.

Connectivity, speed, and intangibles are keeping all of us up at night thinking about our future. To see where they will take us, focus on the constant of what an economy does.

## An economy uses resources to fulfill desires

The only constant is what economies do: again, they use resources to fulfill desires. Their means of doing so, however, have changed several times. Hunting-and-gathering economies lasted about 100,000 years before they gave way to agrarian economies, which endured 10,000 years. Their labor- and land-intensive approach was succeeded by the machines and factories of the industrial era (1760s–1950s), which spawned the growth of cities, mass-production, pollution, labor unions, and the development of the banking system.

After almost 200 years, the industrial era gave way to the computers of the information economy, which is already more than half over. The first four decades used the computer as a crunching tool, an industrial-style approach that included data processing and warehousing, bigger and faster machines, supercomputers, and other "factories" for performing routine brain work.

In this second half of the information era, which we call the BLUR economy, resources will fulfill desires by yet another set of arrangements. One will be that we leave behind the idea of stable solutions. Already, a successful business is neither at rest nor in focus at any given moment. The beginning, middle, and end of a product line are dissolving into each other as the orderly and familiar step-by-step progression of research, design, production, distribution, payment, and consumption disappear. Advance copies of the manufacturers' new model is still being sold at a floating "street" price and the previous version is available at a discount. An annual model changes blurs into a continuous one. Continuous upgrades that are downloaded electronically are replacing model years that require plants to close down for retooling. Built to last now means built to change. Like grandfather's rocking chair, all the pieces may have been replaced over the years, but the intangible – the concept of grandfather's chair – persists.

Like those before it, the BLUR economy has three basic parts.

1. The BLUR of desires – the demand side of any economy – where products and services meld into one to become an offer and where the roles of buyers and sellers merge into an exchange.

2. The BLUR of fulfillment, where strategies and organizations dissolve into economic webs and permeable relationships.

3. The BLUR of resources, where people are no longer divided into their working and consuming selves and where capital is more often a liability than an asset. These resources are shaking off their traditional meanings as vigorously as a dog shakes off water after climbing out of a lake.

# 4

When everything is connected with everything

For every chip that is in a computer there are nine or ten out there that are in more mundane things like toasters, door knobs, and tennis shoes. Computer chips have connected up with each other, now the other microprocessors are doing the same. When you connect a lot of dumb things together and let them interact – communicate with each other – then you get a smart system. This process has barely begun. Imagine the dirty clothes, the detergent, and the washing machine communicating with each other and adjusting their efforts in real time. *Lesson from the Future:* purposefully increase the electronic systems connecting lots of things, as well as people. You have still got a long way to go. Pick an object. What other object would it benefit from by communicating together? Keep expanding the connections.

# Looking to a future of networked embedded processors

Something big is going on right now. Almost imperceptibly – but very quickly – everything around us is getting smart. Our cars are learning to anticipate our moves. Our dishwashers are analyzing the water. Our toasters have stopped burning the toast. Thanks to tiny microcontrollers, we can now buy a blanket with a brain, an intelligent cat litter box, and a learning thermostat. And these are just the beginning. Before long, it will be the assumption rather than the exception that the products we buy will be equipped with embedded processors. We will be wearing them, talking to them, perhaps even eating them.

But if this ubiquity of microcontrollers is big news, it is not half as big as what will come next. Consider that up to now, these things have been fairly content to work in isolation. They focus on the task at hand; they talk quietly to themselves. Over the next few years, they are going to start to raise their voices. They are going to communicate with one another and integrate their activity. They are going to team up.

And where will that leave us?

We have been talking about this question for a few years now. We have seen PCs go from unconnected to connected. And we have seen smart unconnected products. It strikes us as inevitable that the latter will connect up too and that suggests all kinds of possibilities. We think this is a big story and will change the economy in startling ways. In a few spots, it gets troubling – okay, downright scary. But, at the same time, the developments about to unfold are not inscrutable – they are much like ones we have seen before.

# From crunching to connecting

In the early days of the information age, when PCs first entered the scene, they did not exactly set the world on fire. IBM thought there was no future in them and Xerox PARC could not even convince

Xerox there was a market worth exploiting. And then, around 1981, along came two so-called "killer apps" – the easy-to-use applications that would turn the PC into something really useful to the average worker. They were spreadsheets (remember VisiCalc?) and word processing.

Suddenly everyone was running out to get a PC. Its promise as a "personal productivity tool" was bright and sales and production shot up meteorically. However, it was not actually until ten years later that things started getting really interesting. That is because, with millions of desktop computers in place, it suddenly became possible to think about linking them up. It is only through widespread connection that the real promise of information technology is being realized. Consider the first killer app of the networked computer environment, e-mail, which is rapidly evolving into all manner of advanced groupware. And the second, browsing, the popularity of which is leading to the third killer app, electronic commerce. Tools like these do not simply automate unproductive tasks – they change the way work is done. Beyond that, they change the way many of us lead our lives. These are the killer appls after all that are persuading our retired parents to go out and buy PCs – so they can exchange messages (or even videoconference) with their grandchildren. So they can receive information and entertainment based on their interests – not the mass market's. So they can comparison shop on-line. Clearly, what felt like the heyday of the information age a few years back was only a prelude. The greatest use of information technology is not crunching but connecting.

## Cheap and smart

So what does all this have to do with embedded microconntrollers – those "jelly bean" chips now popping up everywhere from greeting cards to lunar explorers? It has a lot to do with them because it suggests the explosion in usefulness that awaits this technology as it follows its own path to connectivity.

Embedded processors are at the same point today as PCs were

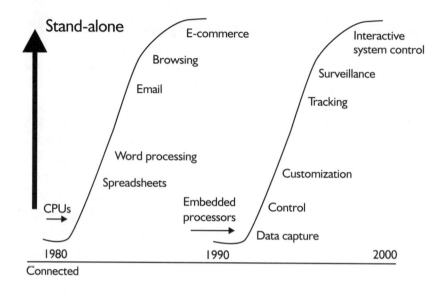

**Figure 4.1** Killer apps for stand-alone processors drive proliferation, which then begs connectivity. Connectivity ushers in new more powerful killer apps. (Source: Ernst and Young Center for Business Innovation.)

during their early, pre-connected days. That is, there are some highly useful and broadly recognized uses for the processors, but still mostly in stand-alone, unconnected modes. What are the technology's "killer apps"? Essentially, there are three. Embedded processors are being used to capture data, control functionality, and customize features. Like word processing and spreadsheet construction, all three are hugely useful functions for a very broad population – and just as word processors and spreadsheet software created a huge burst of interest in PC ownership, these applications are spurring great interest in processor embedding (Figure 4.1).

Data capture is the purpose of much of today's installed base of embedded processors. In Otis elevators, microprocessors religiously take note of every operational occurrence: at what times the elevator is called, how much weight came on board, whether the doors functioned properly. Service technicians download the information for clues on where to focus preventive maintenance. All kinds of other trades now use microprocessors in similar ways. Traffic sensors save transportation department workers the tedium of having to count cars as they go by. Geologists plant sensors along the volcanic rims and fault lines they would rather not walk across daily.

Control is the idea behind many of the other processors embedded in today's products. Heart surgeons put a microcontroller on certain pacemakers to make them capable of defibrillating a runaway heart. Less life-and-death levels of control are exerted by processors in all kinds of appliances and consumer goods. Several of the Canon EOS cameras, for instance, achieve better "point and shoot" results because their eye-control focus sensors can actually perceive where the photographer is looking. They autofocus there, instead of defaulting to the center of the frame.

Customization is the goal behind the embedding of processors in, say, the new Cadillac Seville's "adaptive seat." Once the driver is seated, a computer quickly measures the pressure on ten separate air bladders, each connected to an air compressor. The processor makes adjustments to even out the pressure and ensure a comfortable seat – differently configured for every driver in a family and for the same driver on different days. (In fact, the computer rechecks the data and the seat readjusts itself every four minutes.)

It is not hard to see how the growing awareness of these three applications – data capture, control, and customization – is driving an immense increase in the number of embedded processors. Think about the products your business makes or the services you offer. (Or think about the last five things you spent more than five dollars on.) Would there by any possible benefit in having them adapt, post-sale, to each buyer's usage pattern? Would some form of autocontrol be advantageous? Would it be useful if the thing could capture and spit out an audit trail of its doings? We find it hard to come up with examples of existing products and services that would not be enhanced and competitively differentiated by these possibilities. Now, combine that with the fact that embedded processors add minimally – like, maybe, a dime – to the direct cost of producing a product. Again, it is no surprise they are proliferating. Already, there are about 30 embedded processors for every central process-ing unit (CPU) housed in a PC. We are rapidly building what our colleague John Parkinson likes to describe as "a world of cheap, smart objects." The word is out and the gold rush is on.

One immediate development is that we are starting to notice when products are not "smart." At first, we were surprised by the public rest room toilet that flushed itself or the sink that recognized our presence by turning on its own faucet. How quickly the novelty wore off. Now we find ourselves saying, "Why do we have to handle the paper towel dispenser? Or the bathroom's doorknob?" Embedded processors are rapidly becoming what's known as a "hygiene factor" in products and services. The functionality they allow will soon represent the baseline performance we expect of the things we buy and use.

## Connecting the dots

After the crunching deployment comes the connectivity surge. And driving that connectivity, a new set of killer apps – much more life changing than their predecessors.

Connecting microprocessors, in itself, is hardly the difficult part. Various means to do it exist, all pioneered by the past efforts to connect CPUs. We have at our disposal infrared technology, tele-communications infrastructure, radio frequencies, magnetic fields – any of these can be employed to bring a stand-alone processor into a network. Connectivity also depends on a standard setting: diverse producers and users have to agree on how to make the "hand-shakes" happen. However, again, this is not a barrier; we know how to get these things hammered out.

We can easily make connectivity possible. The only thing wanting is the awareness of the benefits it would deliver. In other words, we know we can do it – we are just not sure why we should care. Once again, it will take a few killer apps to get everyone on the band-wagon. And what will they be? The examples of connected embedded processors we have seen so far suggest a few huge opportunities.

# Tracking

Anyone who has driven a rental car equipped with a navigation systems knows the benefit of tracking capabilities. What is going on here is that a computer onboard the vehicle has been connected to orbiting satellites through a global positioning system (GPS). Essentially, the car transmits a beacon skyward; when three satellites have received it, the computer can fix the car's location within a car length and relate it to the maps stored in its database. As GPS technology continues to drop in price and size it is easy to imagine this kind of tracking will be possible with even small objects – such as a FedEx package or your airport-checked luggage.

GPS gives customers an added sense of personal security because of its tracking capacity. This is also what the LoJack stolen-vehicle recovery system offers, using a different connecting technology (radio frequency). Unlike a normal car alarm, which simply sounds off when it is jostled, LoJack has a way of calling the police. A hidden transceiver on the car allows cruisers in the vicinity to get a fix on the location of the stolen vehicle and retrieve it quickly. How long can it be until PetTrac offers the same capability? PetTrac, if you have not heard, is a product made by AVID Identification Systems of Norco, California, which implants microchips under the skin of household pets in the all-too-likely event they run away from home. At present, the system requires that a vet or animal shelter pass a wand over the animal to retrieve the data on the chip – as of now, it is only capable of recording things like the owner's name and number. When PetTrac is GPS connected, Lassie will always make it home.

Ski resorts are already starting to embed chips in their ski passes, which allows them to track their customers' use of different lifts, trails, and amenities. (How long can it be before they are used to find lost skiers?) Similarly, turnpike commissions are implementing microprocessor-based tracking that charges drivers for their use of a toll road without making them pause at a booth.

Now think about how microprocessor-enabled tracking could change your shopping experience. If it is possible to track even a six-pack of Coke, why have checkout clerks at all (and, more to the point, checkout lines)? We will just "shoplift" everything – and our bank account will get charged automatically by the scanner at the door.

## Surveillance

The darker side, for many people, of connecting embedded processors is the huge potential it will create for stepping up surveillance efforts. Surveillance is already big business, but its high cost has meant that it is used only in limited ways. Connected embedded processors will make it cheap – and pervasive. The first real hint of what is coming is the system created by Net/Tech to ensure that employees who work in restaurants, cafeterias, and other food-handling jobs wash their hands after they use the rest room. As reported in *Forbes FYI* (Winter 1997), here is how it works. An employee's name badge is equipped with chip and a small light. When the employee enters a rest room on the premises, the chip activates an infrared connection with another chip in the doorway and the light begins blinking. It will keep blinking until the employee spends at least 20 seconds in front of a third chip, located at the washbasin. If the badge blinks outside the rest room, it means the employee failed to wash his or her hands – a cause for disciplinary action.

Today, a PC-based product called Kindercam is available for anxious parents who want to check on their children's day care centers. Using a modem, they can see what is going on from their desks miles away. Tomorrow, we will have in-home cameras equipped with motion sensors so parents will be able to watch whatever room the nanny and kids are in.

Is all this a good thing? Certainly many people are nervous about the privacy issues involved. And in truth, it is inconceivable the world will stop at just checking whether you have washed your hands. Who needs Megan's law if every convicted pedophile could be wired to set off a warning when entering a home with children? On the other hand, what parent would not sympathize with the idea of implanting a chip to enable the police to track a lost or abducted toddler? But then again, how many parents would be tempted to leave it in place, just to ease their minds, when Jimmy went off to college? ("Honey, do these sound like the coordinates of the library?")

The upside of surveillance, of course, is increased safety and accountability – and, by virtue of these, greater system-wide efficiency. If fewer resources have to be devoted to double-checking work and catching problems after the fact, more can go into new productivity.

## Keeping up with The Jetsons

If there is an ultimate killer app for embedded processors, it is interactive system-wide control. This is simply the extension of the control applications that stand-alone microprocessors feature; instead of just being purely local and self-contained, networked processors will be capable of collective system-wide control.

A good example is the Sony S-Link system, which connects microprocessors on one component (such as a television) with microprocessors on another (such as a video cassette recorder (VCR)). Shove a tape in the VCR and it "knows" to turn on the television and speaker system and make all necessary compatibility adjustments. Miele ovens are already smart enough to connect with a digital meat thermometer. Normally, a chef has to hover around the oven checking frequently to see if the thermometer dial reads 180 degrees. Miele ovens not only display the data externally – they calculate the estimated time when the oven will reach the target temperature based on the last few readings. What is the next step? Will the oven fire up the burner under the corn at the right time to go to table with the roast? No kidding – this is the world those visionary geniuses behind *The Jetsons* imagined.

More than any other application, we predict, this one will drive investment and use. We will see a boom in the use of connected embedded processors for integrating the activities of different devices. Our alarm clocks, our coffee-makers, our toasters, our blanket – all our most familiar items will start conferring. Our needs will be anticipated as though we were royalty – we will not even have to carry money or keys. And the rapidity with which all this will come about will be exceeded only by how fast we will learn to take it for granted.

This application is already under construction in the industrial setting. Action Instruments, for example, gives every machine and workstation the ability to communicate with the others directly. Collectively, they manage the work flow of a factory. Why is this better than existing systems? Because when something changes at one station, all the others can instantaneously adjust themselves on the fly.

One last parallel between the evolution of PCs and micro-controllers. Once, we thought of computers as hardware. Now, we recognize the value – and the profits – are overwhelmingly in the soft-ware. The same will happen with embedded processors. There will be a high market in microcode to run on these ubiquitous jelly beans.

Two benefits will accrue to any system rich with connected embedded processors: transparency and adaptability. Transparency is a good thing. When UPS puts its package-tracking software on-line, it suddenly made its operations transparent to customers worldwide. It inspired greater overall confidence in its services. Imagine if the location of every Beanie Baby in the Ty distribution network could be pinpointed precisely. Retailers could stop phoning Ty and parents could stop phoning stores. Now, think how it would be to shed light into some really opaque systems, such as health care or public policy making.

Increased adaptability is the even greater benefit of connectivity. With every link that is made and tightened in a system, its ability to capture and act on feedback is heightened. When an event hits the system, the response is more instant and systemic – the entire network adapts quickly to the change. This is true of a shop floor and it is true of an economy.

What has made our country great is our foresight and ability to create infrastructures – such as our Constitution and our market economy – that are robust and flexible enough to support individual initiative and adapt usefully over time. Pushing power downward, away from central processors and achieving order through connections in the system – this approach resonates with our core values as a nation. Our early lead in embedding microprocessors – and now in linking them up – is laying the groundwork for a superior, connected economy.

# 5

## Basic changes in the foundations of wealth

Here, I give you the footprint or architecture for the financial side of the information economy: creating, accumulating, distributing, and controlling wealth for individuals, companies, and entire economies. Each one of these is identifiably changing and will continue doing so for at least the next decade. I will show you, for example, how wealth creation becomes more financial than real all the time, how wealth accumulation shifts from earned to unearned, how the middle class increasingly sees net worth as the source – rather than the outcome – of its wealth, and how control of wealth is shifting from institutions to individuals. All major financial changes. *Lesson from the Future:* the new economy is about more than dot.coms and the Internet; its also about the new causes and consequences of wealth.

*Molecular biologists are up three points and economists down one-quarter in moderate trading.*

*My teenage daughter, a millionaire on paper, is considering going public (but I cannot retire yet).*

*The* Wall Street Journal *reports that 45 percent of the American workforce are free agents.*

Fortune *observes that market indices rather than human resource policies directly determine the compensation of more than half the workforce.*

*The Supreme Court rules that consumers' "clickstreams" (the paths people take as they surf from Web site to Web site) are their private property and that misuse of this information is a federal offense.*

*The last pupil in America is wired – wirelessed, actually – for broad band Internet access.*

*After years of debate, Congress finally passes laws allowing people to decide how much risk to take in their social insurance accounts.*

Labor markets. Wealth. Employment. Management. Property rights. Education. Risk. The old ways no longer hold. New ones tumble in. It is a liminal moment.

The new mantra is "The Internet changes everything" and it is even truer than we can imagine. The foundation of our economy has shifted and with the new foundation has come a new set of rules about wealth. Anything is possible. Even trading molecular biologists.

In fact, the future caught up with us while (originally) writing this page. We had written "The American Medical Association adds day trading to its list of recognized addictions." But then, in August 1999, the American Psychological Association reported that more than 11 million WWW users or 6 percent, "suffer from some form of addiction to the World Wide Web."[1]

You might be asking, "What are Stan and Chris talking about? Investing and trading in humans just as we do in corporate securities? A financial market for human capital? Are they kidding?"

No, we are not. Our economic foundation is changing dramatically and so are all the rules we have about wealth. How we make it and build it, control it, and spread it about are all changing.

We read every day about individuals who start dot.com businesses from their college dormitory, do an IPO (initial public offering) six months later, and become fabulously wealthy (and then the stock plummets). Human capital – your daughter's smarts, a scientist's inventiveness, your knowledge and experience – is the currency of future wealth.

At the same time, corporate America is writing new rules. After a decade of reworking the old ways (reducing, reengineering, rewiring) and now the rush into the new business models for the Internet world, we can next expect significantly new forms of management and organization.

What remains undiscovered, beneath the headlines of me.coms and software billionaires, are the deeper structural shifts in financial markets and in economic value. These shifts are profoundly altering the nature of wealth. By wealth we mean not just the investment portfolios of rich people, but the stock of value that individuals, companies, and societies generate in a successful economy. Wealth means investments in securities, but also taxation, education, industrial plants, and social institutions. To understand how wealth will change in the future, we will start with the past.

## The connected economy

In agrarian times, wealth meant land. In industrial times, it meant factories. Recently, information replaced industrial capacity as the primary means of creating wealth and now the economic foundation is shifting yet again. Today's electronic-commerce strategies and Internet-based businesses are evidence of this happening – they are the current development of the connected economy.

The changes are grounded in the fundamentals of the universe – time, space, and mass. We experience them in everyday life as speed, connectivity, and intangibles. Speed shows itself in drastically shortened product lifetimes, customer response cycles, management decision making, and the end of equilibrium as a management mindset. Connectivity, hooking up everybody and everything electronically, has made distance – space – irrelevant and put any useful information where it is needed, instantly. Intangibles – such as software, information, services, and, more recently, human capital – have replaced hard goods – mass – as the most valuable and fastest-growing part of the economy.

The shift to intangibles happened in three waves. In the first wave, from the 1950s into the 1970s, service businesses grew faster than product-based ones. Services were 31 percent of the US national output in 1950, increased to 42 percent by 1970 and 46 percent by 1980, and reached 55 percent by 1998.[2]

In the second wave, from the 1970s through the 1990s, the core of today's $1.5 trillion worldwide computer and communications industries has shifted from hardware to software and information services.[3] Seen as barely more than an accessory in the 1970s, software now dominates the computer industry and products and services alike are made of and by software.

The third and current wave of intangible value, the rise of human and intellectual capital as the most highly valued resource of the late information age, began in the 1990s and will continue for the next few decades.

These three principles define the connected economy.

1. Speed: constant change is healthier than stability.

2. Connectivity: open systems thrive, closed ones wither.

3. Intangibles: the virtual trumps the physical.

## The nature of wealth

In chapter 3 of this volume, we wrote that the production and consumption of goods and services – what economists call the "real" dimension of the economy – was changing to reflect these principles. Here, we turn to the financial side of the economy. Do not confuse this with the financial services industry, with its banks, brokerages, and insurance companies, although this sector will be profoundly affected. We focus here on the financial aspects of all people, business, and society. We are accustomed to the financial aspects of business. Today, however, as connectivity proliferates, anyone can trade anything of value electronically. Soon every individual will participate in finance – defined as trading risk – as both trader and tradee.

The definition of wealth remains, as always, the means by which we fulfill our desires. As the saying goes, you are wealthy if you want no more than what you have, whether you grasp for frame, fortune, friends, or followers. In economic terms, this translates into material possessions and the means to attain them. In social and political terms, it translates into greater freedoms and the means to attain them. To fare well, we need a new mindset for the way we work and earn, spend and save, plan our mortgages, taxes, and investments, and take responsibility for our own development.

This holds equally for individuals, companies, and societies.

Wealth has a life cycle. It is created and accumulated and then it is distributed, whether through taxation, dividends, or inheritance. At any moment, we can take a snapshot of where wealth is being controlled. Each of these aspects of wealth is mutating.

## Wealth creation and accumulation

While the real economy creates wealth by producing goods and services, the financial dimension does so by bearing trading, and managing risks. This difference is enormous.

For individuals, it is the difference between our labor (real) and our investments (financial). People accumulate real wealth through both their tangible possessions, such as cars, houses, and furnishings and their intangible ones, such as their knowledge and relationships. However, they build financial wealth – their net worth – by bearing risks in their 401(k)s and investment portfolios.

Every asset has a value and every value is at risk. Many of us sell one home and buy another, recognizing that every piece of real-estate has both upside and downside financial risk. Few actively set about trading houses as a way of making profits. More of us, however, are borrowing against our homes in order to trade financial assets based on our judgement of whether they will rise or fall in value. In other words, we trade risk.

For companies, we are discussing the difference between the products and services they offer (real) and the cash flows they generate (financial). Real wealth lies in tangibles, such as factories and in intangibles, such as customer relationships. However, if you want to see a company's financial worth, then look at its share price. That is what companies themselves do and that is why they put so much effort into financial engineering, massaging earnings, and so forth, to keep analysts enthusiastic and investors bullish.

And for societies, it is the difference between the gross domestic product growing annually by 3 percent (real) and the Dow Jones Industrial Average's growing – or shrinking – by 20 percent. It is also the difference between the quality of a society's infrastructure – its roads, hospitals, and the like – and its borrowing capacities and currency reserves.

In all three domains, making money is starting to be as important as making stuff. Money takes on a life of its own. As we have seen in recent history, currency crises can drive the real economy into sharp recessions, as in Mexico, Thailand, Malaysia, and Indonesia. Businesses can be similarly constrained by their liquidity. And individuals save or consume, depending on their own investment performance as well as their appetites for risk.

Traditionally, most economists have considered the real sector primary and the financial sector secondary. In August 1999, this perspective reversed, as Federal Reserve Chairman Alan Greenspan explained to Congress. Here is how the *New York Times* reported Greenspan's testimony:

"We no longer have the luxury to look primarily to the flow of goods and services" when making decisions about interest rates, Mr. Greenspan said. In effect, he was labeling what he called the "extraordinary increase in stock prices over the past five years" as one of the major economic forces capable of pushing up the inflation rate. Traditionally, a run up in stock prices has been viewed as reflecting a strong economy and profitable companies. The economy drove the market. Now the opposite is more and more the case, Mr. Greenspan suggested.[4]

In other words, as we create the connected economy, the economic action – the accumulation of wealth – is shifting from the real economy to the financial, for two main reasons.

In the short term, investors perceive the connected economy as an extraordinary opportunity for creating real future value and are buying into it, bidding up the stock market and creating current financial wealth. There is undoubtedly some inflation of asset values, but the financial markets are correctly recognizing growth opportunities. The rate of growth in value may be temporary, but not the billions of dollars of market capitalization which will ultimately be sustained by the continuing creation of value in real sector.

Longer term, the information economy's form of capital – information, knowledge, and talent – can be leveraged indefinitely at much lower costs than can be financial capital needed to build steel mills in the industrial age. The amount of financial capital required is much smaller, which is lowering the amount of capital needed and, thus, its cost. And, unlike a factory, information's capacity is almost unlimited. The wealth from movies or computer games comes from almost pure margin as more and more people use them, a phenomenon often called "increasing returns."

The connected economy is built on increasing-returns businesses, software most of all and, therefore, takes less physical capital to produce a given quantity of economic value. This is one way the economy becomes intangible. Microsoft's sales-to-physical-assets ratio is 12.26, whereas US Steel's is now only 1.96.[5] This means that financial capital is becoming less scarce, the cost of capital is falling, and the price of entry to new businesses is lower. These factors will continue to hold true whatever the fate of the Internet stock run-up, so do not dismiss them even if, by the time you read this, price–earnings ratios are depressed. To be an entrepreneur, you will not have to create a low-risk business plan to obtain a lot of money. You can create a high-risk one and fund it yourself or with a friend. The ease of raising the required cash or of self-funding new ventures in turn will change the distribution of wealth in society.

## Wealth distribution

Any discussion of wealth invariably leads to the gap between haves and have-nots and future wealth certainly does not promise the end of inequality. But it does mean that, over time, wealth will no longer be just for the wealthy. A major shift in distribution is already beginning within our own minds and our pockets will follow. Instead of standing on the sidelines watching the elite get richer, a broad segment of society will be on the playing field.

Almost all of us know how much we make (income), but it is only a slight exaggeration to say that almost none of us know our net worth. Those who have inherited wealth and the financially enlightened few understand the important difference between income and net worth. They focus on the latter and make it work for them. What they earn directly is not their primary financial concern.

Not too long ago, a lawyer brought this home to us by saying "No matter how much or little you make, it's still only walk-ing-around money." The statement is both arrogant and accurate. His remark underscores the increased importance of "unearned" income and its growing contribution to people's accumulation of net worth. Earned income consists of the salaries, wages, and tips you work for. Unearned income is the additional wealth created by putting your assets to work for you. The more that wealth accumu-lates in the form of financial assets and the more those shares and other securities appreciate in value, the more wealth is created, not as earned but as unearned income.

Unearned income from interest, dividends, capital gains, pen-sions, and annuities has become steadily more important to US households. For every dollar made in earned income in 1975, that is taxable income earned from wages, businesses, and unemploy-ment insurance – US households got 13 cents in unearned income. By 1997, this figure almost doubled, to 25 cents.[6] As wealth becomes more liquid and takes the form of financial rather than real assets, the middle-class appetite for risk is growing. The more unearned income that people make, the more risk they are bearing.

In 1990, investors placed $44 billion in new money into mutual funds. In 1998, the figure reached $477 billion.[7] According to the *Wall Street Journal*, 80 million Americans or 52 percent of households own investments.[8] Paychecks will always matter, bull markets come to an end, financial bubbles burst, and periods of poor stock market performance interrupt the growth of unearned income. But the data suggest an irreversible trend: The source of financial wealth is shifting from money that you work for toward money that works for you. Unearned income is growing and more people have it. Wealth is becoming middle class.

By "middle class" we mean individuals and households not rich enough to live without working, but with enough income to save regularly. Years ago we might have called them "well-to-do." Today, the sustained boom in the USA has moved some poorer families into this category, though the distance between the richest and the poorest continues to grow. In our discussion, what matters most is not the gap, but the proportion of the society we can call middle class and above.

As society as a whole gets richer, people will benefit more from the wealth they previously accumulated and will depend less on their current wealth creation. This feeds on itself. When wealth grows faster than income, unearned income is an ever-larger proportion of total income. To ride this trend, you must appreciate net worth as the *source* of wealth, not merely the outcome.

Wealth has been accumulating for a long time, but even in the advanced economies not everyone is emancipated yet. We are all living off capital generated in the past and most of it is not on the books. Pasteur, for example, accumulated intellectual capital that still reduces misery and lengthens life, but it is not captured in any financial accounting, as if it were fully depreciated and obsolete. As markets get more connected, this accumulation has been building in financial terms and control of it is becoming more widely distributed.

## Wealth control

The control of wealth is tilting from institutions to individuals.

In early industrial times, control of wealth moved from the few landowners to the robber barons who controlled the new scarce resource: credit. In the late industrial era, managers controlled corporate wealth without owning it. Then, the rapid growth of retirement plans and the crunching power of computers made employee pension funds major controllers of the economy's wealth.

Still, neither the employees – those who owned the plans and for whose benefit the pension funds operated – nor the unions – those who helped workers gain their retirement benefits – gained control of the wealth. Instead, control went to the financial analysts who advised the plans and the fund managers who ran them.

With four distinct economic periods (late agrarian, early and late industrial, and early information), we have had four different groups in control of the nation's wealth: *from landed gentry, to owners, to managers, to pension funds.* Now, with the democratization of financial information, individuals are taking more responsibility for managing their own wealth. The power is shifting yet again, this time to you and me. Brace yourself.

Many individuals already have the same on-line access to their retirement assets, whether through their benefits department or e-Schwab, as they do to their Amazon orders and FedEx shipments.

We can safely expect the control of wealth to shift yet again, this time to *individuals,* who will increasingly own and manage their own funds, bear and track their own risk, in order to accumulate net future wealth.

People have become the custodians of their economic futures through vehicles such as 401(k)s, Keogh plans, and individual retirement accounts (IRAs). Individuals, not their employers, are taking responsibility for their futures and managing their pensions is one example.

# Net net

The changes we are talking about are nothing short of momentous. Consider them again.

1. Wealth creation becomes more financial than real.

2. Wealth accumulation shifts from earned to unearned.

3. Middle-class wealth is no longer an oxymoron.

4. Control of wealth shifts from institutions to individuals.

The shift to the connected economy is already revolutionizing the infrastructure of the real economy. And so the ways in which wealth is created, accumulated, distributed, and controlled must change, too. Wealth affects not just the wealthy, but every one of us and every aspect of our society – how we are paid and taxed, what risks our businesses take, how our society invests in itself. Examples are shown in Table 5.1. Future wealth is not just about personal investing. It is about a major transformation in the economic life of individuals, the rules of business, and the welfare of society.

**Table 5.1** Real and *financial* wealth

| Foundations | Wealth creation | Wealth accumulation | Wealth distribution | Wealth control |
| --- | --- | --- | --- | --- |
| **Individuals** | Work and productivity | Household possessions Knowledge Social networks | Last will and testament | Own/Rent home |
| | *Investment income* | *Net worth (401(k), market portfolio)* | *Philanthropy* | *Vested pensions* |
| **Companies** | Production of goods and services | Factories Customer relationships | Pricing | Mergers and acquisitions Capital expenditures and budgets |
| | *Profits* | *Sharehold equity* | *Stock options Dividend payments* | *Stock ownership* |
| **Society** | Gross domestic product/Gross national product Education | Rule of law Public trust Democratic institutions Roads | "Pork barrel" politics *Medicaid* | Property rights |
| | *Stock markets* | *Currency reserves and public debt* | *Taxation Welfare* | *Regulatory controls Bankruptcy laws* |

Wealth has two natures: one real, the other *financial*. For individuals, this duality means the money earned on the job and on Wall Street. Company wealth and society wealth have similar origins. As the table shows, all three constituencies accumulate, distribute, and control wealth of both kinds.

# 6

# From Marx to markets

Trade unions, the ballot box, and socialism are some of the forces that were supposed to improve the workers' lot. None panned out. The last place economists and political theorists told us to look for a successful force was to the capital markets. After all, they create equity not equality. Yet that is exactly where middle-class wealth, no longer an oxymoron, is flourishing. This will continue as we confront another contradiction: talent is today's most important resource, yet labor markets are the most inefficient markets of all. *Lesson from the Future:* The growth of retail capital markets will accelerate economic development globally – and might even be a factor for reducing the gap between haves and have-nots.

*Workers of the world unite.*
*The capital markets will set you free.*

The sheer breadth of ownership of equities in US society today has democratized wealth. According to the Federal Reserve, American households now control, either directly or through mutual funds, 59 percent of all stocks held in the USA, a staggering $9 trillion as of the end of summer 1999. Stocks accounted for only 12 percent of household financial assets in 1990, but 21 percent by 1999.[1]

"America's mutual funds are now worth more than either its pensions funds or its insurers, and are poised to overtake banks as the biggest repository of the nation's wealth,"[2] *The Economist* wrote in 1997. Similarly, in 1998, the *Wall Street Journal* noted that this "phenomenal growth, combined with the flexibility and transparency that mutual funds offer, has given individual investors unprecedented control over America's finance industry."

Another indicator of important directional change is the 1992 Federal Reserve Survey of Consumer Finances, which found that approximately 22 percent of all equities belonged to people under the age of 45 years. That is practically double the ownership of a decade earlier.

## Marx manqué

What businesses call "profits" economists call "surplus." When an economy creates surplus by making something for less than someone will pay for it, the society somehow gives some share of it to the owner of capital and some to labor. In the early twentieth century, as industrial technologies began creating great gobs of surplus in an economy with abundant labor and scarce capital, those who owned banks and big businesses began getting the lion's share of the wealth.

Enter Karl Marx with a relatively simple proposition: owners and workers resembled masters and slaves and the separation between the two would inevitably lead to a one-sided concentration of wealth and a plutocratic economic system. The broad mass of labor that built the pyramid would always bear the load, not the lucre. Marx argued to reintegrate worker and owner, giving the people control of the means of production, taking property out of private hands and giving it to the state. In a democratic society, all the people would share property of the state.

Marx's theories fell to Leninism, Maoism, Stalinism, Nazism, and *perestroika*. Far from dispersion among the people, power and wealth under these systems converged in the ruthless hands of the state and its bureaucrats. But the corruption of the theory did not necessarily disprove the underlying thinking.

As early as the 1920s, many others in the industrialized world tried to redress the same social and political problems or economic disintegration and the growing wealth gap between owners and workers. Through the trade union movement, workers sought a collective voice to balance the power of the owner class and to bring their adversaries to the bargaining table. As unions gained strength, the share of surplus that flowed to labor grew. Remember, though, that many owners who viewed powerful labor as a threat to private property fiercely resisted unions in the USA.

The union movement could not have succeeded without the ballot box. Where democracy held sway, voters and their representatives consistently used non-revolutionary political means to pursue equitable economic ends. In the USA, the progressive income tax, estate and capital gains taxes, and social security began to redistribute the fruits of ownership. Today, the Employee Retirement Income Security Act, the ingenuity of the financial markets, and the arrival of the connected economy all broaden and deepen ownership. Financiers are freeing today's working class through a portfolio of equity investments in productive private companies.

A century ago, capital was a scarcer resource than land or labor. Today, the scarce resource is talent – intellectual capital, not financial capital – and information technology is the means of production most likely to create wealth. Neither is capital intensive. A few talented people can create a lot of value with a very affordable amount of information technology. One result could be a tremendous accelerator of economic development in the underdeveloped world. Another will be the redistribution of power in the developed one.

In an autocracy, despots abuse or suppress talent, whereas in a meritocracy, talent roams free and can rise to the top. In a plutocracy, robber barons exploit ideas, but in a democracy the idea itself has worth and its owner can convert it to product and broadly distribute it at a relatively low cost. That is where we are today.

In a democratic market economy, all of us already own our own intellectual capital. It is our private property from the get-go. This did not matter too much to the ditchdigger of 1990, but is crucial as knowledge workers become more important. As companies of one, individuals hold their own capital assets. As ever, of course, talent is unevenly distributed across individuals. However, the efficient human capital markets enable the talented to find their best use and hold on to their fair share.

Entrepreneurs lead the way, particularly in Silicon Valley, where fortunes are made almost overnight. When these billionaires turn philanthropic, they invest in social capital, as did the Rockefellers, Carnegies, and Mellons.

The bigger story involves not the creation of wealth by the growing new entrepreneurial class, but the distribution of wealth. As we have grown richer, we have begun to save more, first investing in homes and now accumulating financial assets. Uncle Sam helped with tax breaks, subsidized loans, and legislation establishing tax-favored pension vehicles, such as 401(k)s and Keogh plans.

The disparity between the top and the bottom 10 percent may distract you from the 80 percent in the middle. Look closely: median family income has grown a little more than 1.5 percent annually. Despite complaints in the 1980s of a stagnating middle class, family income grew in constant 1997 dollars from $20,102 in 1947 to $44,568 in 1997.[3] This income is being turned into financial wealth. Pensions have migrated to automatically vested contribution plans which individuals keep with them as roll-overs when they change jobs. Stock options spread ownership of the means of production ever more broadly, particularly in knowledge-intensive areas such as Silicon Valley.

Instead of separating workers and owners, the connected infrastructure and the financial sector of the economy are aligning the interests of enterprises and their employees – who are increasingly the owners. At the same time, 401(k) and other wealth-generating plans are aligning workers' interests with the interests of the whole economy. Furthermore, legislation altered distribution and the capital markets are doing so even more.

Capital markets create equity, not equality. However, when the capital markets make ownership and wealth from intellectual capital and when those financial assets reside in the individual, then the balance begins to tip toward larger numbers of people. When that happens, instead of concentrating at the top, wealth begins to spread broadly through the ranks. It just may be that capital markets distribute wealth more equitably than anyone previously imagined possible.

## The super rich are irrelevant

"If all the superrich disappeared, the world economy would not even notice. The superrich are irrelevant to the economy," Peter Drucker said in *Forbes* in 1997. "The combined sources of money from retail investors, pension funds and retirement plans of all individuals is the fastest-growing source of money. The most important source of capital is the average mutual fund transaction of $10,000."[4] Drucker elaborated his point in *Wired* the next year. "The rich no longer matter," he said. "They're celebrities, not capitalists anymore. The real capitalists are the middle-class people who put $25,000 into a mutual fund."[5]

The only money Andrew Carnegie's employees saw was their wages and few owned any stock. In contrast, Bill Gates has made an estimated one-third of Microsoft's 30,000 employees millionaires through the company's employee stock option plans. In his 1996 book *The Road Ahead*, Gates said that one of the purposes of going public in 1986 was "to provide liquidity for the employees who had been given stock options."[6] The cars and housing prices around the company's hometown of Redmond, outside Seattle, showcase the shifting balance between income and financial assets, but not as clearly as this remark of Roxanna Frost, leadership manager at Microsoft: "We speak at Microsoft of the day when an employee calls in rich."[7]

## A better way to motivate

If one company can produce 10,000 millionaires, then could 1000 companies come up with 100 different ways to make 10 million millionaires? Probably not, because most companies are not as pivotal to pioneering a new world as Microsoft has been. But suppose that the *Fortune* 1000 undertook the challenge to enhance the net worth of their employees – 50 to 100 might succeed and another 100 to 200 might have partial success. Along the way, they could all become laboratories of new and unique approaches to wealth creation and distribution.

Even though other companies do pursue the Microsoft way of distributing stock, most corporations, particularly large ones, still prefer to hold the bulk of stock options for the chief executive officer and a few other select executives. They reward the majority of their employees primarily with a salary. Then they spend hundreds of millions of dollars on motivational programs. A much better idea: align the interests of owners and employees, reward the best workers sufficiently that they begin to think like entrepreneur-owners, and give them a stake in the whole and not just a bone from the part through employee stock option plans and other increasingly popular stock purchase programs.

The gap between haves and have-nots remains all too real. Wealth is pooling at the top alarmingly and not every distribution of wealth will trickle down to those who need it most, in the USA or around the world. Still, control of wealth steadily migrates to a broader number of individuals. *An intangible knowledge economy is inherently more democratic than an economy based on tangibles, because ownership of the scarce resource is in the hands of the individual.* It is still true that brains are unequally distributed, as is access to educational facilities where minds can be trained and broadened. But we can take encouragement from some innovations. The capital markets are finding ways to help democracy work.

## Narrowing the gap with microlending

The Internet community's 1999 INET conference in San Diego, where rich-country interests vied with poor-country concerns, highlighted these issues. Africa, with 13 percent of the world's population, has just 1 percent of the world's Internet users.[8] The gap in access to capital is now about access to intellectual capital.

How do you close or even narrow the gap when, worldwide, not one person in 100 has a computer? By building relative wealth. Even the super poor can mobilize a financial net worth. However, minuscule, microlending programs of various forms provide both financial and human capital to those who most need it around the world. A women in Bangladesh who raised chickens borrowed enough to rent a cellular phone so that she could check chicken prices in neighboring villages. She evolved into a local telecom provider, earning twice the average wage and her livestock became a profitable sideline.[9] "Give a man a fish, and he eats for a day." These programs teach people to fish and they eat for a lifetime.

A number of groups, including the International Labor Organization (ILO), a UN agency based in Geneva, sent missions to Colombia, Iran, the Philippines, and other countries to study employment growth in the "sandal economy." The idea was to start with small capitalizations and, in the words of Hla Myint, a Burmese economist at the London School of Economics, to "let the market work."[10]

Compared to traditional economic development assistance, this meant betting less on central planning and constant top-down control and more on market-supervised, bottom-up entrepreneurship. It also came to mean spreading risk through offering microcredit, often only a fistful of dollars at a time, to any number of individuals.

Significantly, it also meant a change in viewpoint. These programs looked at the poor who benefited from these economic initiatives as nascent businesses rather than as disguised underemployment.

If a peasant woman in India prepared hot food at home and brought it to her husband at work, then the ILO encouraged her to cook for a few more workers as a service business. The ILO oriented those who developed a small enterprise to hire one or more others. What began as a job growth strategy became microbusiness growth, with jobs and wages as outcomes.

By themselves, microcredit programs and the resulting enterprises obviously do not turn poor countries into rich ones. Judged by the criteria of financial lending, however, they have been successful: more than 90 percent of borrowers paid their loans.[11] The Grameen Bank in Bangladesh launched its first microcredit program 20 years ago and now enjoys a repayment rate of over 95 percent on more than $2.4 billion in loans. Grameen makes a profit on microlending.[12] Pressure from borrowers helps. The microentrepreneurs are clustered in small communities to create both mutual support and powerful peer pressure. Default on your load and you freeze the credit of everyone else in the group. The borrowers form a kind of risk-taking commune.

By the late 1990s, microcredit programs had reached 15 million people living on a dollar a day or less, the poverty line as defined by the World Bank. Of those people, 13 million lived in Asia.[13] Microcredit leaders have established the ambitious global goal of reaching 100 million people by 2005, still only a fraction of the planet's 1.6 billion impoverished people. To reach that target, moreover, the would-be lenders will have to expand dramatically into Africa, where only approximately 1.2 million of the estimated 300 million now living in poverty are currently in microcredit programs.

The poor are often suspicious of taking on debt, but it is risk aversion that often stands in the way of wealth creation in poor and rich countries. Although microcredit programs could reach many more borrowers, a great number stay away from debt, forgoing the risk – and the potential rewards.

In Chile, for example, capital markets support social innovations ranging from microlending to 401(k) plans to government-sponsored investment programs. Nations engage the energy and contribution of poor and not-so-poor alike when they put surplus in people's hands through the capital markets rather than the state.

## Future wealth expectation

The growth of retail capital markets will accelerate economic development globally – and might even reduce the gap between haves and have-nots.

# 7

## Basic changes in the three largest sectors of the US economy

When the foundation of an economy changes, you should expect to see major shifts in the operating models of every sector in that economy. In an original article for this volume, I show you what this means in the three largest sectors of the US economy. Health care (# 1) will shift from treatment of diseases to prevention and prediction; today it is caught midsteam in the transition that Americans call "managed care." Education (# 2) will also shift. During the change from agrarian to industrial eras, the education mantle moved from church to state; this time it is moving from the public to the private sector. Defense (# 3) is also changing: see how the conduct and meaning of war is different in agrarian, industrial, information, and the future bio-era. *Lesson from the Future:* the basic model for your sector of the economy is changing as we speak; will you be among the first or last to know what it is becoming?

Change the foundation and you change the entire edifice. This is as true for economies as it is for buildings. When the foundation of an economy shifts, so too does the basic business model for every sector of that economy. The chapters that you have read so far in *Lessons from the Future* have detailed the changing foundation. Now, we examine the major paradigm shift this is causing in the three largest sectors of the US economy: health care ($1 trillion), education ($665 billion), and defense ($270 billion).

# Health care

Until only a decade ago, health care was really sick care or, to put a more positive spin on it, *medical care*. Medical care was built on a model that emphasized not heath but disease. Paradoxically, doctors had a moral responsibility to keep their patients healthy, but while you were healthy you never saw your doctor. Not until your illness was far enough along to convince you that you needed to see your doctor; only then did they intervene. And, it was customers (patients) who initiated the medical interventions.

*Managed care*, the transitional health care model the USA is now passing through, took the medical care system and flipped it almost entirely around. Before, the sick care industry made money by filling hospital beds. Under managed care, the industry makes money by emptying them. Colloquially, you might say, this is a shift from horizontal care to vertical care, get them out of the beds and hospitals as soon as possible. This is still not about preventing illness. Under managed care, so the theory goes, prolonged illness is failure, neither a medical nor an economic opportunity.

Has managed care changed health insurance? Dramatically. Has it controlled costs in the process? That too and controlling costs was its first and foremost mission. But has it changed the delivery system? In fact, very little. All it has really managed to do is relegate delivery to the back seat, while health insurance gets the steering wheel. While managed care has shifted the value creation focus from producing goods and services (caring for the sick) to a financial focus (reducing medial delivery costs), in both instances, the focus is still on risk as a problem rather than on health as an opportunity.

True *health care*, a model that is only beginning to emerge, will only mature as the connected economic foundations mature. Patients more and more will become, in effect, their own doctors. Risk in medical care is lodged upstream with providers, doctors, and hospitals and in managed care it migrates a bit downstream to payers, the insurance companies. In the connected era of real health care, it will migrate progressively downstream to patients. But with risk will come reward, the chance to become a lifelong monitor and caretaker of your own well-being. Doctors and insurance companies see managing risk as a problem to minimize and control, whereas consumers will see their health care risks as opportunities to maximize and proactively manage in order to create value.

Under managed care, power has migrated from large central hospital facilities to smaller neighborhood clinics and health maintenance organizations (HMOs). In the new health care model, it will continue to migrate further from the center and into the home itself. This is made possible by connecting technologies that are stepping forward to fulfill new market needs. Home products that allow consumers to test themselves for everything from pregnancy to blood sugar counts, prostate-specific antigens, and vitamin and mineral deficiencies, for example, will continue to flood into the marketplace.

Through connectivity – intranets, extranets, the Internet and World Wide Web – patients are already forming themselves into electronic support groups. Today, those groups deal most often with chronic and catastrophic illnesses, as well as end-of-life issues, but the use of the Internet in coping with medical problems and enlarging health knowledge will continue to expand. As it does and as people have more and more capacity to diagnose and analyze themselves at home, power within the health care system will shift from providers to payers to customers. Remember, the infrastructure technologies of the information era are distributive not concentrating.

In spatial terms, the home is only the penultimate place "Doc" will move. Ultimately, in the bio-economy of the future, doctors will move into our bodies in the form of implantable medical devices that will allow continuous, real-time monitoring of patients from remote stations.

Pacemakers are one such device. For years, if something went wrong with a pacemaker, the patient had to call the doctor for an appointment and clear it and subsequent adjustments with their insurer, a process that could take a worrisome week or more. Since 1973, Medtronics has made a pacemaker that a computer analyzes by phone. Soon, the computer will both read the pacemaker and adjust it – on-line, in real time. Soon, too, even proximity will not be an issue. Medtronics makes another implantable, Gem DR, that can be continuously read by a wireless monitoring box. Today, patients have to be within 40 feet of the box, but wireless is wireless. Some day in the not distant future, geosynchronous tracking will allow patients to be continuously monitored and adjusted anywhere on earth.

As the locus of power migrates from provider to payer to consumer, value and, hence, wealth will migrate to the businesses most ready to empower consumers medically, just as it had migrated under managed care to those businesses most ready to put the payer in charge. Changes in the health care sector have not occurred with Internet-economy speed, but we can see that, in approximately two decades, surely by 2020, we will have passed from medical care through the transitional managed care into true health care.

## Education

The cycle of change has been far slower in education, the second largest sector of the economy. However the impact of the shifting infrastructure on changing the basic model is also working here just as surely.

During the agrarian era, the church and the family shared the major responsibility for education. Church was where the widely scattered farm communities gathered, whereas home and family were central both socially and economically. Where schools did exist, their schedules reflected farm schedules, with time off for planting and harvesting. Learning in the schools was simple and undifferentiated: the youngest and oldest children shared the same teacher and space.

As society shifted from agrarian to industrial worlds, schools and schooling shifted along with them and the mantle of responsibility for education slowly passed from church to the state, that is mainly local government, but also state and federal. Over the course of approximately one century, from the American Civil War to the Second World War, the one-room rural schoolhouse gave way to the brick and mortar urban classroom. Teaching itself became highly specialized – with separate degrees for elementary and secondary education and separate tracks for college preparation, general education, and learning the trades. Within the classroom the industrial model applied. Students sat in rows reminiscent of factory assembly lines, with a boss–teacher firmly in charge at the front.

However, the shift to Internet connections is finally beginning to move education into a new model for how to create value. Who will inherit the mantle of responsibility for education in the connected, lifelong era? The answer is simple: people will be educated formally by the institutions where they spend the most time. That means schools for the first two decades of life and, thereafter, as an employee in the workplace and as a consumer in the marketplace. In this redefined market, the largest segment in dollar terms – students – ultimately becomes the mature and declining tertiary market segment. Employee learning is the growth segment and consumer learning – still only in gestation – is, nevertheless, potentially the largest education market of all.

The value creation shift is for the private sector to see value and, thus, wealth in assuming the educator's mantle. That is beginning to happen and entrepreneurial leaders are seeing how to make money in this newly embraced role.

We predicted this shift in *The Monster Under the Bed* in 1994 and, in 1996, the privately held firm Knowledge Universe (KU) was born with a $500 million investment from three partners: junk bond king Michael Milken, along with his real-estate tycoon brother Lowell and Larry Ellison, the billionaire founder of software giant Oracle. Our bets are on KU as the type of company most likely to forge the new model for creating educational value in the information era. KU identified 31 segments they wanted to be in, from pre-school to retiree education, from CD-ROM tutorials to textbook publishing, and from executive training to learning toys. KU went on a buying spree and, by mid-1998, had more than $1 billion in revenues.

KU has a hypothetical market value of $4–6 billion, approximately eight times the principal investment. If KU doubles its hypothetical value to $10 billion then goes public with an IPO value of, for example, $15 billion, it would be large enough for institutional investors to take a position in. Once that happens, it will set off an alarm bell that what has been a very fragmented for-profit educational industry is consolidating.

In another five to ten years, it is hard to imagine more than three or four principle players, for example KU, possibly an entertainment company such as AOL Timer Warner, Walt Disney Corporation, or Bertlesmann, each of which have brands highly transferable to education, and perhaps a software and professional services giant. No doubt companies of this scale, for better and for worse, will be picking away at the big dollars in the public education arena. The USA spends $665 billion per year on education; $446 billion of that is in public education, that is kindergarten to adult, and $219 billion is private or for profit.

The transformation to electronic age education will grow faster in the private and for-profit sectors first. There it will blend traditional lessons of growth, scale, and consolidation with lessons from software economics of the connected era, such as increasing returns and shrinking costs in virtual delivery systems. In contrast, public education rejected telephones and televisions in classrooms and, while it is now accepting PCs and the Internet in classrooms, the absorption rates will still be far slower than in the for-profit markets. The private sector will capture the for-profit educational market first, then the lessons will permeate into public sector education.

Whether public education survives as the dominant "kindergarten to university" model in the long run remains to be seen. The historical record suggest that, fourth quarter, declining monopolists seldom bootstrap themselves into the future based on a totally different model than the one they dominated for decades. As with church-based education the last time around, public schools will more likely hold onto the old model, eschewing risk and continuing to lose market share to new entrants such as KU who are better at applying the new technologies to education.

Here are two examples of what it would take for public schools to redirect their mindset; still stay public but do so while embracing the new and larger educational market. I will use post-secondary public education, because I am most familiar with that.

First, colleges can only admit so many students because they are locked into brick and mortar delivery systems. In this model, if they improve the quality of their offering and more students want to attend their school, then they will be in the "enviable" position of admitting one out of every ten instead of one out of every four. From the business perspective, this is absurd – the better you are, the more customers you can turn away? With electronic delivery systems there is no need for that, even in the public sector.

Second, despite the now widely accepted notion of lifelong learning, most colleges kiss their students goodbye once they graduate. Except, of course, "do not forget to sent us your alumni check." This violates another basic trust of business – that it is better to keep a customer than to have to find a replacement. Since most post-secondary students go to school within 100 miles of their homes – four-year research universities with national admissions pools are the numerical exceptions – why not admit students with the mindset that you will make them your students/customers for life? That is true value creation and very possible in today's connected world.

# Defense

Connectivity creates new sources of value, in warfare as much as in education and health care. If defense and the military, the third largest sector of the US economy, is your business, you also are headed for a profound redefinition.

The mission of defense is to protect the nation and, to do that, the defense forces have to be prepared for war, the purpose of which is to cripple the enemy's productive capacity. In the agrarian economy that meant burning the fields or, if the stakes were high enough and the conflict bitter enough, salting them. In the industrial economy, you crippled the enemies productive capacity by bombing the factories. Because these were in the cities and because bombing was remarkably crude by today's measures, that meant you bombed large numbers of civilians.

In the information era, it is the information infrastructure that needs to be wiped out – radar installations, communications systems, anything that can talk to one another or talk to the enemy to tell them where you are. It is not by accident that, in the Gulf War, Baghdad itself was largely spared while communications centers were pounded. That the hottest topic today in defense circles is biowarfare can hardly be surprising, even though the bio-economy is still gestating. Like every other business, making war goes where the economy's dominant technology goes.

The faster the technology of war changes, the faster and, therefore, the shorter warfare becomes. In the agrarian era, wars lasted as long as 100 years; information traveled glacially – by horseback or carrier pigeon at best, by foot at worse – and massed armies faced off on open fields. The industrial age brought us wars measured in a decade or less. By the end of the age, the products of industrialization – planes, tanks, armored ships, and submarines – had spread battlefronts across the globe and into three dimensions. By then too field telephones and other communication devices had dramatically reduced the time it took information to flow from the front to command headquarters.

In the information era, the tactical goal is to use both the crunching and connecting infrastructure to know where everything and everyone – from tanks, planes, ships, artillery, infantry, and ammunition, to logistics and the customer (read, enemy) – is at every moment. Digitalized maps and laser range finders have reduced the time-lag, between citing a target and destroying it with a mortar, from eight minutes in the Vietnam war to approximately three minutes today. That means less ammunition, fewer supplies, less cost, and far fewer logistical problems as a result.

In the Second World War, US tanks required an average of 20 shots to locate and finally hit a target. By the 1973 Israeli war, technology had reduced that figure to 12 shots. In the Gulf War, on the world's first digitalized battlefield, US tanks needed on average 1.4 shots. The differential competitive advantage for a tank today comes less from Detroit, where the tanks are built, than from Silicon Valley.

In theory today, it would be entirely possible to fight an electronic war, engaging the enemy without ever sending in a single soldier or tank. However, that is a coin with two sides. At the heart of the US military infrastructure are millions of computers and tens of thousands of local area networks. Just as we could attack an enemy without sending in soldiers or planes, so terrorists could stage an electronic Pearl Harbor, attacking the core of our economy without every engaging our military. In the most securely locked chambers of the Pentagon, the CIA, and the National Security Administration this will come as no surprise. The defense and military establishments are in a very different business than they were in only a decade ago.

The common threads in all the changes described above are the shift of the location of control from the centers (be they hospitals, schools, or command and control centers) to the peripheries, the shift from concentrating infrastructures to distributive ones, from centralizing institutions to decentralizing ones, and the substitution of financial and physical capital with intellectual capital.

When financial capital was in short supply, it was fully absorbed by the needs of the real dimension of the economy. Financial capital was the bottleneck for wealth creation and that fact made the financial dimension of the economy subservient to the real dimensions (see pp. 63–4). Today, in the developed economies, there is more financial capital than our intellectual capital can put to efficient use. There, the financial capital is freed up by ever leaner inventories and more efficient and cheaper factories, racing around the globe in search of opportunities for creating wealth. The financial dimension of our economy is no longer absorbed by the real dimension and it is taking on a life on its own. It is the ever weightier tail that is wagging the ever leaner dog.

As with these three largest sectors of the economy, so with every other sector and every other business. What applies to health care and education applies equally to professional sports or leisure wear; what is happening to defense is fundamentally no different than what is happening to food processing or transportation. As the foundation of the economy moves from crunching to connecting, the definition of what constitutes value in each field is shifting. Riches go to those who foresee and lead the shift. It is happening everywhere.

# Part III

Business

# 8

## Informationalizing every business

"Informationalizing." An unfortunately inelegant word for a notion that can transform any business and give it an entirely new life. The idea is that every business has information buried in it or in its customers that could be useful for invigorating it – so useful, in fact, that the new information can even become more profitable than the original core business that produced it. The era of dot.com businesses did exactly that: using information as pure play, they deliver goods and services in a way that old line companies had to scramble to imitate. Even with the bursting of the dot-com bubble, established businesses will have to learn this new way. *Lesson from the Future:* informationalize!

The intermediaries of the industrial economy, such as real-estate agents, are often displaced or their functions are transformed when businesses are informationalized. Their demise is paralleled by the rise of new-age "infomediaries." Infomediaries are enterprises that use the various forms and functions of information to link buyers and sellers electronically.

Infomediaries can also link producers and consumers, those upstream and downstream, providers and users, and senders and receivers. They add value by enabling these parties to obtain better and quicker information from one another. With convenient and direct access 24 hours daily, they deliver real-time results in order to meet customer needs. Infomediaries are superior to traditional intermediaries that offer more expensive, time-consuming, and limited fare. They furnish a wider range of options than the traditional services do because they consolidate information unavailable from any other single source. Rather than going through lengthy and multiple steps, they handle inquiries, processing, and transactions all at once. They facilitate customized transactions and can preview outcomes of any selection or decision. Informationalized intermediaries or infomediaries will create and provide these services to participants in all businesses within a generation. Those businesses that do not informationalize within that time in all likelihood will be out of business.

Like the leaders of the businesses of the industrial economy who built their empires by laying railroad tracks and highways, the creators of the new infomediaries are building their empires on electronic tracks that will direct the movement of an industry's information. And now that the computer and telecommunications infrastructure is being constructed, the race is on to establish dominance in the info-businesses. For the next 15 years or so, the third quarter of this information economy, each major business sector will experience the proliferation of information channels, followed rapidly by a shake-out and finally the consolidation of a few leaders among these enterprises.

Fragmented channels will give way to one or two dominant infomediaries in each industry. These leaders will provide the primary electronic distribution pathways for the most profitable slices of business, the information services. The new infomediaries will ultimately represent the principal means of access for buyers and sellers in all businesses by the time the information economy matures, that is before 2010. Participation in these electronic channels inevitably will become necessary and virtually all firms will be represented on the dominant systems.

## You can informationalize virtually any business

When any relatively standard product becomes an electronic blip on a computer screen, the fact that the blip represents a cow or a car becomes virtually irrelevant for the purpose of a transaction. When the bank held our home mortgage in yesterday's economy, it literally stored the document in its vault. Today's mortgages are written so that they can be packaged and sold as securities. Mortgage blips are now commodities, trading units to be bought and sold over and over in secondary markets where they are hedged optioned, securitized, and cleared. Economist Robert Kuttner pointed out that, while the ultimate in deregulation occurs in Third World bazaars, where every price is negotiable, consumers in advanced countries rely on posted prices. With custom products and open electronic markets, prices also become customized. However, the possibility of gouging disappears as electronic markets expand the scope of offerings and vendors.

Computer systems have introduced periodic airfare adjustments and the electronic marketplace is pushing us toward continually adjusted pricing. Imagine gas pump prices electronically linked to world oil prices. Or available airplane seats and theater tickets whose prices drop in order to clear the perishable inventory as the scheduled times draw near.

In vacation travel, a potentially large market exists in finding last-minute buyers for unsold and cancelled vacation packages. Sellers list last-minute opportunities that are about to go to waste and vacation buyers who are willing to go on short notice wherever the bargains are can scoop up huge savings.

There are probably similar opportunities for developing a secondary market in returned and rush concert, theater, and sports tickets in large cities. Since the value of the original product is about to evaporate, the added value of the infomediary may well be worth more than the item sold. Data banks for vacation condo time-shares use the same principle. This kind of electronic marketplace could create computerized trading of tickets, rental cars, and hotel rooms. Secondary and futures markets are likely to develop for a wide array of products and services.

Remember, between now and 2005 the information infrastructure will be completed and virtually everyone will be connected. Between now and 2020, literally tens of thousands of specialty markets may appear. Videotex provides electronic malls for entrepreneurs to set up shop alongside giant retail chains. Those who do well will offer many traditional benefits, such as convenience, lower cost, and more choice. They will also offer 2020 features, such as faster response, ease of use, more processing capability, mass customizing, and previewing of future outcomes.

Think of open electronic markets as two-way classified advertisements. Anyone can list items for sale in the want advertisements and anyone can contact a seller directly. Electronic want advertisements extend the function of classifieds even further through query and matching services and by providing broader geographic coverage if desired.

## An 80–20 rule for the 2020s

These developments are likely to occur in the maturing quarter of the information economy. What will company profiles look like by the time we enter the final, aging quarter of the economy? What will be their probable revenue and profit mixes between their traditional and informationalized businesses? What will be the market value of each? By 2010 many if not most companies will have so blended these old and new businesses that the distinction will be more analytical than real. But peering at the future from midway through this economy, we see a profound change. The average firm will shift its focus from industrial-age products, services, and channels to new info-business lines and distribution channels. The new info-businesses will include services that provide turbocharged information, industry-wide product offerings preview, 24 hour access, and self-design features, and many of these services can become stand-alone businesses in their own right.

When we distinguish between core businesses of the old generation and informationalized service businesses now, new-generation lines rarely account for more that 25 percent of revenues or profit. The 80–20 rule in business states that 80 percent of your business comes from 20 percent of your customers. It takes the remaining majority of customers and a large organizational overhead to contribute the residual 20 percent. An information-age variant of this rule would be that, by 2020, 80 percent of business profits and market values will come from that part of the enterprise that is built around info-businesses. Mature non-informationalized businesses and, again, large organizational overhead will account for 20 percent or less (see Figure 8.1).

|  | Revenue | Profit | Market value |
|---|---|---|---|
| The old-generation core businesses | 80% → 50% | 50% → 20% | 80% → 20% |
| The new-generation info businesses | 20% → 50% | 50% → 80% | 20% → 80% |

**Figure 8.1** Predicted shift in business patterns 1990 → 2010

If the greater economic value is in the secondary, information dimensions of the businesses, why not shift resources and management attention to those activities? Just such a process began during the past decade. A few far-sighted people in a few large corporations crafted such visions. They were going to create the megacorporations of the future, synthesizing a revitalized core business and a bevy of new-generation, information-based service businesses. The colossus providing one-stop shopping for all financial services, the combined plane–hotel–car rental–travel company, the advertising–consulting–accounting urge to merge, and the integrated communications leviathan are all examples of visions that have foundered.

The dreamers always rush to put the vision into place through merger and acquisition within a couple of years. Few survive. In the rubble and aftermath, there lingers the sense that maybe such visions will come to pass in the distant future. But for now the better part of wisdom perhaps refocuses on the core business, buttressing it with the internal growth of related information businesses. Many of these are still embryonic; a few are growing rapidly. In the long run, those that succeed may ultimately supplant the core. But until then, they will be seen and treated as support players whose major job is to insulate the corporation when the next down cycle hits again.

In the decade of the 1990s, we got balance more than succession. The technology, infrastructure, and market were not yet prepared for much more. One or two decades from now, however, turbocharged information activities will become the primary businesses, while what used to be primary may even be sold. The business cores in today's economy are like parents in their forties and fifties with offspring who are young adults. Ten years from now, the older generation will start retiring and the younger generation will come into its own. But that is for the 2010s, the last quarter of the economy, not the third quarter we are in now.

The new generation of businesses do not overwhelm us as revenue producers in the short terms, even though Wall Street analysts assign them a disproportionate share of companies' break-up value. These businesses have evolved from cost-saving efficiency moves to value-added services to customers and then to tiny business lines that keep on growing. They are the turbochargers, not the main engines and, although their returns can be extraordinary, in their early growth years they were still infants, big enough to survive but too small to be at the center of management's vision for the future.

When they reach around 30 percent of the total corporate profits, however, their quantitative heft will produce a qualitative transformation. By that time, the savvy players will know this trend will continue and accelerate. They will no longer be simply turbochargers. They will be generating their own power and, as management focus shifts to these new businesses, new principles and perspectives will move to center stage in the corporate mind. That will signal a profound transformation not only in the way an organization views the business world, but also in how it views itself.

# 9

Smart products and knowledge businesses

Data, information, and knowledge are three increasingly important levels of expression. Data, the most elemental, is how we express things and it dominated in the 1950s and 1960s. In the 1970s and 1980s we elevated data to information (from "data processing" to "information technology") by focusing on applications and the meaning of the data. The 1990s introduced the next level up, knowledge, defined here as the practical use of the information, and the custom continues into the 2000s. This excerpt demonstrates how to add value to any enterprise by building it into a knowledge business. *Lesson from the Future:* what do you know that your customers do not and vice versa? Connect up, start the knowledge flowing, and apply it in real time.

# Any business can become a knowledge business

Where is the Life we have lost in living?
Where is the wisdom we have lost in knowledge?
Where is the knowledge we have lost in information?
T. S. Eliot, Choruses from "The Rock," I
(*Collected Poems 1909–1919*)

Long before there were computers, T. S. Eliot linked information, knowledge, and wisdom. Since then many people have fine-tuned this progression, added data (as in "Where is the information we have lost in data?"), and turned the sequence around from loss to gain.

The result is a four-step progression from data to information to knowledge to wisdom. Data are ways of expressing things and information is the arrangement of data into meaningful patterns. Knowledge is the application and productive use of information and, finally, wisdom is the discerning use of knowledge. Each step does not necessarily lead to the next, but they must be taken in proper sequence to achieve the final goal.

Data are the basic building blocks of the information economy and of a knowledge business. They are the way we express things and group them together. Or, as Robert Lucky, a former director of AT&T Bell Labs, says, they are the unorganized sludge of the information age. In this economy we focus on data that come to us in four particular forms: numbers, words, sounds, and images. And their functions or what we do with them include creating them, manipulating or processing them, moving them around, and storing them.

Random numbers are data; a random number table is information. Sounds can be thought of as notes (data) and, when arranged in some system, as music (information). Depending upon the skill of the composer and performer, the result can be greater knowledge or even wisdom for those who listen and learn. In mathematics the building blocks are numbers and, through processes like addition, subtraction, multiplication, and division, we create meaningful patterns of information. Algebra and geometry organize the information into bodies of knowledge. In language the building blocks include nouns, verbs, adjectives, and adverbs or (more generally) words that, when arranged in meaningful patterns, become information. These in turn may take the form of literature from which knowledge and wisdom may stem.

As they apply to the economy, data, information, and knowledge have life cycles and such cycles are usefully divided into four quarters: gestation (Q1), growth (Q2), maturity (Q3), and decline (Q4). Data's economic importance was embryonic in the 1950s and 1960s and entered a growth quarter in the 1970s and 1980s. In the third quarter of the cycle, data are now a commodity. In the fourth quarter of the cycle, a few decades from now, data will become a utility like gas or electricity, which you simply plug into and are charged for usage.

Information is a quarter turn after data in life cycle progressions. Its economic importance was recognized only about a decade ago and it is still in the growth phase of its cycle. One day it too will mature. What will take its place? Behind it in the queue, gestating right now, is knowledge. The economic importance of knowledge is still in the first quarter of its life cycle, poised for take-off and accelerated growth in the years immediately ahead.

An intuitive way to appreciate the difference between information and knowledge is to substitute the word *data* every time you see, hear, write, or speak the word *information*. Chances are that there will be an emotional resistance. It will not feel right. It is going backward and it strikes us against the grain. In business, for example, *chief information officers* are much bigger wheels than *data processors*. The latter are not even officers. Data now are widgets, commodities, just not as powerful or prestigious as the information derived from them.

Within a decade we will feel the same kind of resistance in talking about information and information-based tools. Knowledge and knowledge-based tools will have greater power and appeal. Information-based products and services will have lost a lot of their buzz, not because they were a fad, but because they will have been superseded by a more powerful and useful generation of offerings. The value of knowledge will supersede the value of information, just as the value of information took over from a focus on data.

We are only beginning to understand what the knowledge age is all about. We do know that future growth for mature businesses comes from advancing level by level, from data through information to knowledge and that any business can transform itself into a knowledge business. Furthermore, any business offering knowledge-based products and services, whether it realizes it or not, becomes a learning business. The business itself must continually learn how to provide that product or service and customers become learners through the use of knowledge-based products and services. Knowledge businesses are not limited to brainy folks in education, to nerdy folks in "high tech," or even to any folks who employ only smart people and sell only to smart customers. Rather, every business has the potential to become a knowledge business, one whose greatest value is derived from the knowledge that has become an intrinsic part of its offering to the marketplace.

Every customer also has the potential to become a lifelong learner. The provider implicitly says to the customer, "You get smarter when you use my product, because you not only get the thing itself, but you also learn how to use it in a more powerful and enjoyable way than its pre-knowledge-based ancestor. My product educates while it serves."

In the world of business, words like "information," "knowledge," "education," and "learning" are often used interchangeably and without definition. While "education" has been badly pilloried in the past few years, "knowledge" and "learning" are currently positive and popular. We hear phrases like a "knowledge worker" and "learning organization," but they have been used so facilely and superficially that they almost lose their meaning. Buzzwords produce muddy thinking and, in reality, there is a significant difference in the meaning of the words *education* and *learning* as they relate to the four steps to wisdom and to business (Figure 9.1).

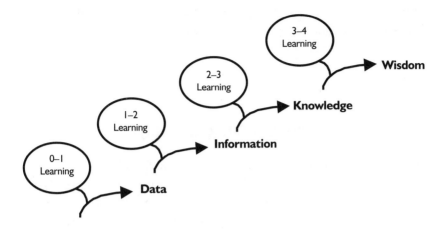

**Figure 9.1** Four steps to wisdom

In the four steps to wisdom, education is instruction and mastery at a given step to level and learning is the movement from one level to the next. Schools teach education more than they teach learning. Businesses have to avoid this trap. To serve as an information or knowledge business that will educate its customers, a company must first learn, then enable its customers to learn in successive steps.

Each step up in learning requires a new technology platform. Computers enabled us to take what might be called the "0–1 learning" step up and ushered in the data age. They required lots of training and thousands of people used them. The marriage of computers and telecommunications was the basis for the "1–2 learning" step up form data to information and it brought us into the information era. By this stage computers required relatively little training and millions of people used them.

The technology platform that will make possible the "2–3 learning" step up and usher in the knowledge age is the blending of computers and telecommunications with human actions. By the time the knowledge phase matures, around a decade from now, billions of people will use computers with no training at all. Can we imagine the technology platform that will enable us to take the final step to wisdom?

# The knowledgeburger

Any product can become a knowledge product and any service can do the same. How, for example, could you turn a hamburger business into a knowledge business? Starting with the basic learning steps we outlined, let us first establish some basic hamburger data: its ingredients, for example, such as protein, fat, and carbohydrates and their varying functions, such as nutrition, convenience, price, and aesthetic pleasure. When you put the data into a meaningful pattern, the information you derive tells you both the menu and the market – in other words, what business you are in.

The next step is to learn from the information, so that hamburgers become a knowledge business and, in addition to getting tasty and nutritional food, customers can make use of knowledge about that food. When customers place orders for an entire meal, for example, can the calorie and fat count be calculated and printed alongside the items on the bill or even at the time of order? What, then, is wisdom in the hamburger business? Perhaps in addition to taste and price, it is learning to eat the right food.

Can the same be done at a supermarket? When customers buy halibut steak, for example, they could flip electronically through a dozen recipes for halibut preparation, print one out, and pick up the additional ingredients at the same time. The knowledge here is about the product rather than literally built into the product itself. Still, even a supermarket can add value by adding a learning component to the products it sells.

Selecting television programs can also become a learning experience. With over 100 channels now to choose from and 500 to 1500 on the way, viewers need to filter and select. Simply flipping channels is selecting from data. When these choices are organized into lists, as in *TV Guide*, they become information. If the program guide is listed on a television channel, shifted from paper to an electronic form of delivery, it is still an information-based product.

An interactive electronic program guide, however, would have the potential to become a knowledge product. If you do nothing more than control the speed with which the choices scroll in front of you, you are still using the guide only to get information. But once you can interact with the material being presented, you could put it to much more productive use. If you could ask for all the television programs this week that are comedies or are about pollution or cooking fish, then you have elevated the information to knowledge. The wise use of that knowledge is up to you.

When information can be sorted by any desirable criterion, you may use it to transform your television set into a learning device. It is then only another small leap to say, Why just a week? Why not all programs on pollution over one year or more? Why not smart filters that can scan past, present, and future programs for you, creating a video library on demand, according to the categories you select? And where will the smart filter be located, in the electronic television guide of the future or in the future television set itself? The resolution of such questions will bridge the gap between television and education as we have known them, making education and even entertainment into true knowledge businesses.

The Federal Communications Commission's 1992 decision to allow telephone companies to transmit television programming is making electronic program selection and much more a reality. The fiber-optic and/or wireless digital networks on which they run will not be in place for about a decade. When they are, both schools and business, students and consumers, will be able to roam through remote electronic libraries, offering everything from missed soap operas and movies to research references and medical files. Dialing up a video-service menu using the combined technologies of telephone, television, and computer blurs the distinction between consumer and learner.

Monthly bills can also be turned into knowledge products. Billing summaries, as for credit cards and telephone calls, can be pretty boring and confusing affairs. American Express was the first to distinguish itself from its competitors by separating one year's worth of customer transactions into categories useful for tax and business purposes. The individual charges are data and the monthly bill is information, but a billing summary organized by category becomes a knowledge tool when it helps you control travel expenses and prepare your tax form.

Some credit card companies do this for a nominal fee at year end, but why not extend this with monthly and year-to-date displays as well? And while they are at it, why not offer a menu of other variables according to which the data can be displayed? Or, for a one-time charge of five dollars, would you like your monthly bill to organize charges by category (food, travel, entertainment, and so on) rather than by date? How about in the format of your organization's travel and expense reimbursement forms? Some knowledge businesses can be built around fee-based services that give customers choice about how information can best be put to productive use.

Knowledge products and services will have relatively short life cycles. It is hard to keep them proprietary. In commercial banks, for example, foreign exchange advisory services are very knowledge intensive. Wealthy clients often have global investment portfolios and need advice on how to handle the risks of hedging or speculating on their foreign exchange exposure. This kind of knowledge is subjective and the ability to systematize it has not caught up with the rate of increase of knowledge on managing such risks. In some senses bankers want it that way, because high profit margins are associated with new knowledge. As you are able to make the knowledge systematic, the margins deteriorate.

Patent protections on intellectual property are still not nearly as developed as they are on "hard" technologies. So the half-life of proprietary information is short, unless you can find ways to build barriers around the knowledge built on top of the information. This is where advantages of scale enter in. If you are a big competitor, you probably know more about a market than the small players. The managerial challenge for those running foreign exchange advisory services, a knowledge-intensive business, is getting their professionals in New York, London, and Tokyo to share their knowledge. When that knowledge is systematized and widely shared, however, it will become available even to the small players.

# 10

---

# What is your emotional bandwidth?

As information becomes cheaper, attention span becomes dearer. How do you get people's attention in the Internet age? One answer is to engage them emotionally and experientially. Information technologies are making this more and more common. *Lesson from the Future:* using information technologies, you can engineer emotion without being manipulative and you can experience feelings in all business communications.

In the old way of doing business, emotions never had a very legitimate place. The industrial age emphasized rationality and machines – including computers – never had emotions.

Make room for the new way of doing business: information technologies are going to make emotions a regular feature. Why? The more information becomes an infinite resource, the more attention becomes a scarce resource. And the best way to get attention is through emotions.

Today all computer applications are based on four basic forms of information: numbers, words, sounds, and images. Of the four, sounds and images have a much higher emotional valence than do numbers and words. Yet the only two major PC applications so far have been spreadsheets and word processing. No killer applications yet for voice, music, photos and videos.

They are coming. The image processor Adobe Photoshop, for example, is well-known among photographers and designers but not by the general public. Imagine if software like this were as universal as word processors. Would it not change the way people communicate as radically as did the telephone and the modem?

None of this would be possible without the huge gains in computer power and bandwidth we are witnessing. The dry word "emotions" takes up a mere eight bytes on your hard drive. A miniature color photo – one inch on its side – that might evoke an emotion would run 4000 bytes. One second of color video, complete with sound, would raise the ante to 1 million bytes.

But think what you could do with those bytes. Environmentalists successfully use emotional arguments to gain attention, whereas their targets typically make the mistake of being stone-cold rational. Companies like Monsanto, Exxon, and McDonald's would be smarter to fight fire with fire, adding emotional interfaces to rational content in order to present their case.

I have in mind a Web site with questions and answers on environmental policies – with the answers in the form of sound and pictures.

Such a site would not get a lot of hits today because conventional telephone lines cannot handle multimedia with acceptable speed.

But the Internet is evolving. As the price of bandwidth comes down, computerized sounds and images will become as important to every business as numbers and words are now.

Some corporations are already pushing technology to the limits. Fidelity Investments is one of those, with an application that does not demand a lot of bandwidth. The fund purveyor handles 575,000 calls per day, 75% of which are automated. In Canada, the company is piloting a voice-recognition system that can recognize spoken English and French. Callers can ask for the net asset value of the funds they hold and obtain quotes on other funds.

Take another example. United Parcel Service (UPS) has scored with its electronic signature receipts, in use since 1987. It was a *tour de force* on UPS' part to capture these signature bit maps and transmit them via wireless links into a package-tracking database. A John Hancock takes up five to 20 kilobytes or one to four kilobytes after digital compression. How might competitor Airborne Express leapfrog this technology? Move up the voice signatures. (So far neither of them is contemplating such a feature.) Now we are talking 100 kilobytes. As computer networks and memories get more capacious, that is quite doable. I expect to see the photograph identification on credit cards reinforced or replaced with voice recognition or fingerprint imaging technology within five years.

Madison Avenue and Hollywood are pretty adept at using computers to create nifty visual effects. Is it not time these skills seeped into the rest of business? Imagine, for example, bringing emotion-rich technologies to the tens of thousands of meetings, presentations, speeches, conferences, and events taking place in the corporate world every day. Clip art is shifting from static frames to video clips and will be joined by clip music in standard display and demonstration software. Goodbye to boring bullet-point slides, hello to sound bytes. Ernst & Young has used network television-quality video clips to help win competitive multiyear, multimillion-dollar consulting contracts.

Corporate annual reports have gone from just-the-facts-ma'am 10-Ks to full-blown multimedia shows. Cisco Systems and Schlumberger, for example, issued their annual reports on interactive CD-ROMs. What is next: interactive, video-rich annual shareholders' meetings. For better and for worse, you can bet there will be a lot more emotions there.

You have heard the expression "look and feel." It used to refer to the screens you got from your spreadsheet software. It is going to take on a new meaning. Computers are going to look at you and feel you.

Electronic sensors and interfaces provide new ways for man and machine to interact. I will take it a step further and predict that computers will someday detect and transmit odors.

It is not as ridiculous as it sounds. Remember that soot sniffers – otherwise known as smoke detectors – have been in mass production for a long time. Technologists like California Institute of Technology Professor Nathan Lewis are using electrical conducting polymers to develop an electronic nose on a chip.

Smells will be created electronically, perhaps with a disposable palette of chemicals deposited into microscopic wells on a silicon wafer. When we have that, it is a short step to two-way smell interactions over the Internet. One day, companies will register odormarks together with their trademarks. Picture the twenty-first-century dating game on the Internet: "Do you want to go on a date?", "I don't know, e-mail me your smellprint."

Similar electronic technologies are being developed for computers to see and touch. As each of these computerized senses becomes further refined, as well as combined, the emotional bandwidth of the network increases. Think of what it could do to sales presentations. Oracle now demonstrates its police database using a siren sound whose high-decibel blare grabs your attention in ways that no spreadsheet can. E-mail will graduate from primitive "emotions," like ":-)," to angry voices, calming sounds, and sensuous scenes.

Emotional bandwidth will become an enabling technology that will manifest itself in software, in interfaces, in search engines, on WWW pages, and in computer and communications architectures. It's coming from the most unemotional of disciplines, engineering, and it is being built into the entire range of information technologies. As this happens, silicon will enable us to express more completely who we are, as people and as businesses.

# 11

## Mass customizing

Mass customizing is a simultaneity of opposites. Applied to business it means the production and distribution of customized goods and services on a mass basis. Since I coined this term in 1987 it has entered into common usage but, I believe, has still only begun to realize its potential. Technologies continually broaden the potential for further application. This trend will continue and grow in the future, as in the way genomic technologies will one day allow the mass customizing of prescription pharmaceuticals. It is not a buzzword de jour. *Lesson from the Future:* elements of every businesses' products and services can be mass customized, as can their markets and organizations.

As the new economy matures, many new concepts, theories, models, and frameworks will develop that are appropriate to actual conditions, not hold-overs from the industrial economy. One seems particularly ready: mass customization.

Let us begin with mass customizing shirt manufacture. Any shirts produced at one time and with the same specifications are parts of a single whole production run. Producing one custom-tailored shirt means the whole has only one part; the production run in the factory may mean the whole equals 5000 identical parts. What if technology made it possible for every one of the 5000 shirts to be customized while on the factory assembly line, that is to say produced just as quickly as the 5000 identical shirts, yet at no greater expense? Each shirt then is both a whole and a part of a whole at the same time.

The world of mass customizing is a world of paradox with very practical implications. Whether we are dealing with a product, a service, a market, or an organization, each is understood to be both part (customized) and whole (mass) simultaneously. New technologies are now coming on-stream that deal with infinitesimal parts of the wholes that interest us. They are able to get specific about parts that earlier technologies had to leave undifferentiated. In addition, they operate at such fast speeds that we may consider their treatment of parts simultaneous. Speed and specificity are the hallmarks of these new technologies and the foundation for the mass customizing of the products and services that follow. Speed and specificity enable us to see how the whole is actually present in each one of the parts.

## Biotechnology and genetic engineering

Biology is a field where technological breakthroughs increasingly permit mass customizing. In the nineteenth century Mendel formulated the theoretical principles of genetics. From these we know that genes determine heredity, though the structure of the genetic mechanism was not discovered until almost a century later. The current biological revolution began with the discovery of the double helix stucture of DNA by Crick and Watson in 1953. Since then, biologists have understood how biological characteristics are transmitted and they have proceeded to engineer life forms by acting directly on the genes. In terms of our basic progression, biotechnology and genetic engineering are about to move from technology to business, from research and development to (customized) mass production. A major part of this development is the highly customized and mass-produced miracle drugs.

In agrarian economies, the local healer or a household member would custom blend a batch of natural herbs and medicinals to heal a sick person. In contrast, industrial economies learned to produce healing drugs in enormous volumes. Remembering that the US industrial economy spanned 1865–1945, however, the early drugs that were mass-produced were multipurpose. Patent medicines, as the joke was told, would cure most everything that ailed you. As the modern pharmaceutical industry grew, it produced more specific medicines for specific diseases and in very large quantities.

The earlier generations of remedies were woefully hit-or-miss, as were the methods for discovering them. Finding a new drug pretty much meant trying tens of thousands of chemicals until you hit on the right combination. Even then, the new drug generally attacked the disease, not the fundamental cause that lay more deeply buried in molecular biology.

Today, however, scientists are able to get at the specific substances – the enzymes, hormones, and factors – regulating cell functions and pathways. One or more of these specific substances is deficient in a diseased person and molecular biologists assume that, if there is activity (or is not activity where there should be), there is a gene controlling that activity that can be identified. Once identified, specialized enzymes snip out the relevant pieces of DNA. Substances that occur in infinitesimal quantities in the human body can then be produced in large amounts. These scientists virtually walk up and down the gene looking for sites to engineer. The path begins in the micro-universe, where breakthroughs in science lead to technological applications and, ultimately, to the mass customization of drugs – new products for the industrial sector of the new economy.

A prime example of mass-customized drugs are the magic bullets know as monoclonal antibodies. Antibodies are the first line of defense against infection. In the 1970s British researchers discovered a way of fusing an antibody-secreting cell and a cancer cell. The outcome produced large quantities of the ultrapure or monoclonal antibody that seeks out and locks onto a specific target, killing only the cancer cells without harming healthy tissue.

Drug makers are now testing large numbers of such products. Johnson & Johnson has an antibody that blocks white blood cells that destroy transplanted organs. Other companies are taking aim at a variety of cancers, multiple sclerosis, and "hospital acquired infections" that cause 80,000 deaths annually. Multiple sclerosis is caused when a specific kind of white blood cell that normally attacks bacteria goes haywire and strips the protective sheaths of nerve cells. The magic bullets destroy these specific white blood cells.

The first vaccines, against smallpox, was developed in 1778 by Edward Jenner. Although there have been only ten widely used vaccines since, the mass customizing of drugs has produced approximately 20 others that are currently being developed. Among those that may win Food and Drug Administration approval in the future are vaccines for AIDS, chickenpox, cholera, croup, viral diarrhea, dysentery, gonorrhea, infectious and serum hepatitis, genital herpes, malaria, meningitis, rabies, strep throat, typhoid fever, and tooth decay.

Traditional vaccines inoculated the person with the killed or weakened virus or bacteria, causing the recipient to form antibodies. The problem was that it also occasionally caused the disease it was intended to prevent and sometimes had side-effects that were worse than the disease itself. The new vaccines, however, are so targeted that they significantly lessen these dangers.

There is even talk of a cancer vaccine. Today, the best cancer treatment is to catch it early and remove it surgically. However, attempts are now being made to synthesize and produce in quantity little-understood substances of the immune system. Research at Genentech is attempting to bond gamma interferon, which seems to suppress tumorous cell growth, with tumor necrosis factor, which seems to destroy tumors already there. Ultimately, cancer prevention may come from the other route to mass customization. That is, isolating the specific gene that may trigger the uncontrolled growth of tumors and develop monoclonal antibodies in large supply.

Truly significant drugs are also expected from "protein engineering," that is modifying specific chemicals of the body, then mass-producing them as synthetic compounds that selectively block disease processes. Because they are synthetic, they cannot be broken down by the body; therefore, they can be taken orally because the digestive system will not destroy them.

The technological key to customized molecules lies in computer modeling that also uses holographic techniques. Sophisticated computer graphics, like those developed at the National Institutes of Health, instantaneously show researchers how a drug reacts with a body protein at the molecular level. With these kinds of tools, molecules are being designed the ways cars and jet engines are designed today. The result is customized molecules, mass produced to fight and prevent disease.

When dealing with the fundamental transformation of an economy, it is essential to grasp the abstractions on which it is premised. However removed these may appear to be, ultimately they derive from our understanding of the fundamentals. The basic abstraction of the new economy, which we have focused on in this chapter, is the simultaneous existence of mutually contradictory phenomena.

A clear drawback of the industrial-based paradigm, on which the notion of economies of scale is built, is that it requires us to operate under the constraints of an either–or bind. In this model, either goods and services are produced in small volumes, in which case they are customized but have high unit costss or they are mass produced, in which case unit costs are brought way down but high volumes make customization impossible. In the economy of scale model, it is not possible to custom tailor products and services and, *simultaneously*, have the voluminous, uninterrupted production runs that are necessary for low costs. You can have one or the other at the same time, but not both. Our models are still built around false dichotomies that say you cannot have it both ways, wanting your cake and eating it, too. Some managerial either–ors are given in Table 11.1.

**Table 11.1**  Managerial either–ors

| Either | Or |
| --- | --- |
| Centralized | Decentralized |
| Headquarters | Field |
| Staff | Line |
| Strategy | Operations |
| Planning | Implementing |
| Important | Urgent |
| Task oriented | People oriented |
| Corporation | Individual |
| Cost | Quality |
| Process | Structure |
| Level | Span |
| Flexibility | Order |
| Specialization | Integration |

New models, therefore, have got to overcome this either–or dilemma and deal with the simultaneity of business opposites. The simultaneity condition says that we must accept the coexistence of mutually contradictory phenomena without trying to resolve the contradiction. In the either–or dichotomies of an industrial paradigm, this is not possible. As in the example at the beginning of the chapter, a shirt is either custom tailored or mass-produced. We have seen, however, that the new technologies will permit customized manufacture on a mass basis. Rather than being limited by the paradox, they seem to embrace and transcend it.

The power of the hologram lies in the fact that, if the image is broken, any part that remains will reconstruct the whole! For this to happen, all information about the whole must be present some-where in each part. This unique property is unlike the mechanical paradigm of the industrial economy, in which the whole is merely the sum of all the parts. Rather, all information about the whole exists in each and every one of its parts. This is comparable to the fact that the entire human genome exists in every cell of the body, except in red blood cells.

If the whole exists in every one of the parts, as well as in the sum of them, then what space does the whole occupy? If the whole is everywhere, it is equally nowhere. The whole has no space dimen-sion to it. If this is always so, if it occurs all the time, then the whole has no time dimension either. If the pattern of a holograph has no time or space dimension, it exists only in frequencies, whose trans-formations are experienced as objects. This is a bizarre world, not the one we experience regularly. Yet it exists, as part of the universe.

We know this to be true scientifically and technologically. Is it also true for business and for organizations? Currently, the answer has to be only somewhat, but becoming more so. Remember, these are the last transformations to take place and each one raises the paradox in a philosophical way. Until the seeming contradiction is accepted in our technologies, it will be difficult to embrace it in our businesses and organizations. And we are still grappling with the technological causes of the paradox.

Medical technology, for example, can keep a patient alive under extraordinary circumstances, creating ethical and legal debates as to when a person is truly dead. If the heart or brain is "dead" yet the body lives with mechanical support, is the person alive? Only parts of the person are alive, yet many take this to mean that the (whole) person therefore lives. When families permit donor organs of the deceased to be implanted in others, a part of their loved one goes on living. Moreover, every cell of that donated organ (part) contains the entire genetic foundation of the departed. Does the whole exist in the part?

This is a fundamental abstraction, manifested in science and technology. If we can grasp it, it will be a powerful key to our understanding of society, of business, and of organization, which ask the same sorts of questions.

Can it be said with equal possibility, for example, that the entire family resides in each member, that the entire army resides in each soldier, and that the entire corporation resides in each employee? Can it also be said with equal possibility that the entire corporation resides in each of its products and in each of its services? Certainly, from the customers' point of view, this may be true.

Technologies are bringing us toward more complete paradigms with which to build our businesses and organizations. The shift from a mechanical to a holistic paradigm is occurring in science and in technology. It is logical, therefore, that it will move next into our constructs of business and of organization.

# 12

---

# Capital: possession is nine-tenths of yesterday

The information economy changes the meaning of all elements in business, and capital is no exception. The type of capital used, how it is valued, and who focuses on it, for example, are all changing. The rule of physical assets has yielded to financial income, which is, in turn, yielding to intellectual growth as a new foundation. In consequence, we learn to value what moves not what is standing still, to use it and use it up rather than own it, and to value intangible assets over tangible ones. *Lesson from the Future:* ask what financial and physical capital is on your balance sheet?, how fast are you using it?, and might it do more for you by belonging to someone else?

# What is capital?

To understand what is blurring in capital, some definitions and historical perspective are in order. Strictly speaking, the term *capital* has always referred to the accumulation of productive capacity. In other words, it is the enduring infrastructure that must be built, acquired, pulled together, and maintained to support production of a stream of goods or services for consumption. Most of us, when we think of capital, think of two things. First, we envision factories, machines, warehouses – all the stuff Karl Marx called the means of production. Second, we think of money, the financial backing required to set up those capabilities.

The earliest form of capital would have been purely of the physical nature, stone axes in the Neolithic economy or seed corn in the agrarian economy, for example; in other words, capital goods and not financial capital. Prior to the early feudal times, the Western world had only so-called subsistence economies, which were hardly economies at all. There was battering – I might give you one of my pigs in return for so many days of your carpentry services – but such activity produced no surplus in the system. Sure, a great harvest one season might produce a surplus, but whatever could not be eaten would only rot in the next. There was no way to convert what was left into enduring form. Without surplus, there could be none of the accumulation that constitutes productive capacity.

Feudal economies represented an early arrangement that allowed surplus to be extracted from the activities of laborers, then accumulated. The key was that feudal lords had a way to convert the surplus into durable form. They took the tithes they received from serfs and used those goods to pay the laborers, who otherwise would have been at work in the fields, to build their castles and cathedrals.[1] Those monumental edifices were the accumulation of surplus value and became the capital that neighboring lords most wanted to grab as a way to expand their won domains.

It was not until we entered what is known as the craft and guild economy that financial capital became a pronounced feature of the economic world. At that point, the level of labor specialization had reached a point at which simple bartering could not supply a family with the goods it required. Striking the complex three- and four-way deals that would convert horseshoes smithed in the morning into chicken on the table that night would have taken all day. Coins were struck as convenient tokens of value storage – another, more fungible way to accumulate economic surplus.

This was a fortunate innovation, for when the technologies of the Industrial Revolution came along, vast amounts of capital were required. It takes more than a village's tithes to build a Bessemer converter or a catalytic cracker or an assembly line. This is why the so-called robber barons of the nineteenth and twentieth centuries – the Carnegies, Morgans, Mellons, and Rockefellers, for instance – were as tied up in banking as they were in railroads, steel mills, and oil fields.

By the end of the Industrial Revolution, when factories and machines were the embodiment of capital, the financial system had grown into a full-size shadow of the world of physical capital. No longer viewed as a token of value, money had value unto itself. People perceived that the accumulation of surplus did not have to mean converting those tokens into physical capital. They could accumulate surplus themselves and place it into storage facilities like banks or stocks. With the development of banking, they could even borrow against accumulated surplus. Financial institutions like banks and insurance companies began to proliferate and financial capital, the shadow or derivative, took on a life of its own.

This is where we are now – almost. Interestingly, financial capital is such a presence today that it casts its own substantial shadow, a derivative of a derivative. The system of information that supports financial transactions has now matured to the point that it is seen by many as an even better receptacle of accumulated surplus value.

Perception is the key. Capital continues to change its appearance or guise and has come to mean different things to different people at different times. Yes, capital is a constant in that it represents and accumulation of productive capacity. But physical and financial capital now have company as "intellectual capital" begins to emerge.[2] It, too, represents the accumulation of productive capacity, but the realization behind calling anything intellectual capital is to acknowledge that our most valuable assets and our most enduring means of production are knowledge, talent, and experience.

## Value what is moving, not what is standing still

What becomes a corporate legend most? It used to be that a solid balance sheet was the most accepted indicator of enterprise value. The measure of a company's greatness was its asset base, made up of all the land, buildings, equipment, and inventory it owned outright. The balance sheet added up all that property, alongside all existing claims against it. Like a snapshot, it portrayed the position of the business accurately and in a way that all interested parties could easily comprehend.

However, like a snapshot, the balance sheet reported on just one point in time. It told nothing about trends upward or downward; it gave no context in which to assess future prospects. In many cases, it painted a much more sanguine picture than was really the case; a company's top accounts might be defecting left and right, its workforce might be out on strike, but still the company's value looked intact. Just as often, companies were short-sheeted by their balance sheets. A firm with a groundbreaking product might be experiencing brisk, high-margin sales, but thanks to debt taken on during research and development, might look like it was nearly bust. Imagine you owned the goose that laid golden eggs. The balance sheet would report holdings of one goose, but it would assign no value to future expectations and, thus, miss the point.

It has only been in the past half-century that most business people have realized it is more useful to focus on flow and change rather than on stock and stasis. With this realization came the rise of the income statement as an indicator of enterprise value. The income statement, of course, is a sort of elaborate footnote showing how the company arrived at the "retained earnings" line; a "stock" concept, not a flow, in the balance sheet. Whereas the balance sheet shows balances as of a specific date, the income statement shows the flow of activity and transactions over a specific period of time. As such, it depicts the true health of the business in a much richer way. Future accumulation of value, it becomes clear, is more closely related to income than to assets. As a consequence, debt began to rise as a proportion of equity, because a company was not priced for its net worth – a measure of the capital it owned, free and clear – but for the income it could generate. Return on equity replaced return on assets as the dominant measure.[3]

Now the focus is shifting again. People analyzing enterprise value are more concerned with future prospects than current performance. The change is most apparent on Wall Street where the valuations of firms are reflected in their share prices. No one has missed the fact that those prices are yielding market capitalizations for many firms that far exceed their book values. On average, the market capitalization of a company quoted on the New York Stock Exchange is two and a half times its book value. An investor simply would not arrive at those values by focusing on the flow reported in the income statement (much less the stock reported on the balance sheet). Is Wall Street suffering another attack of irrational exuberance? No. It is just that, when it looks to determine value, Wall Street does not focus on assets, nor does it focus on income. Instead, investors search primarily for a promise of growth.

Table 12.1 summarizes how the methods of valuing a company have shifted over time, attempting to clarify further the shift through analogies from physics and mathematics. Again, as business people attempt to assign a value to a company, they can focus on its assets, its income, or its growth rate. These are, respectively, expressions of stock, flow, and acceleration. By analogy, picture yourself at the stock car races placing a side bet after the gun has gone off. You could look at the relative positions of the cars at the moment. Probably this is not too useful, since it is still early and the one who was in pole position has a deceptive advantage. Better to focus on the relative speed of the cars at the moment you placed the bet. However, if you could gauge it, the really useful factor to know would be their relative rates of acceleration. It is the car that is picking up additional speed at the fastest rate that is most likely to win. In

**Table 12.1** The blur of capital

| Type of capital | Valuation focus | Who focuses on it | Economic concept | Physical analog | Mathematical analog |
|---|---|---|---|---|---|
| Physical | Assets | Auditors | Stock | Position | Number |
| Financial | Income | Analysts | Flow | Speed | First derivative |
| Intellectual | Growth | Venture capitalists and simulators | Acceleration | Acceleration | Second derivative |

mathematical terms, the shift is from focusing on a simple number to focusing on a derivative of that number and then to focusing on a second derivative of the original number.

Yugi Ijiri of Carnegie Mellon recognized this shift early; for the past decade, he has been refining a proposed addition to the standard set of financial statements. The purpose of the addition is to depict the momentum of change in the company (that second derivative). He refers to the system he is constructing as "triple-entry bookkeeping" because his acceleration statement would inform the income statement as much as the income statement informs the balance sheet.[4]

## Getting capital in gear

What does all this mean for capital in the blurred world? First, if you use your own capital, and it shows on your balance sheet, accept that capital in the traditional sense is a false god. It does not make sense to stockpile great amounts of physical assets for their own sake. They have little intrinsic worth. We have often heard that a human body, as valued by the sum of its elements – mainly water with particles of a few semi-valuable chemicals – is worth approximately two dollars. The same applies to companies: asset ownership bestows little credit, it is what you do with them that counts. At rest, they rust or decay and ultimately end, as does a human body, as dust. Put those assets in motion, however and you create living value.

Second and more importantly, this means that every bit of capital you do own should be kept not only in constant motion but at an accelerating pace. The faster capital works, the less of it you need. The point applies to physical capital as well as to financial capital. It is only in systems where inventories sit unproductively on shelves that everyone needs a lot of them. This means, for instance, that if you have the ability to cut and sew leather, you should not become a captive resource of Nike, but rather should create an economic web of your own for New Balance, the Tannery, Hermès – whomever – so that you can keep your capital equipment in constant motion (connection) and learn from each of the businesses you serve (intangibles).

When matter accelerates toward the speed of light, it picks up mass ($E/c^2 = m$). In the same way, as income goes around faster and faster, at some point it takes on the economic weight of capital. Hence, you can borrow on the promise of an accelerating income stream as Marimba, Mainspring, and countless other Internet start-ups have done. That is why, if you own a securitized form of human capital, such as David Bowie bonds, you will be able to leave a chunk of his income stream to your heirs. *When you decide to own and manage capital, value what is moving, not what is standing still.*

## The blurring of capital goods and consumption goods

The easiest way to understand the difference between capital goods and consumption goods is to understand their yin and yang: capital goods are the physical capacity that enables the production of goods for consumption. Traditionally, it was easy to tell the two apart because consumption goods were ephemeral, while capital goods endured. The detergent you bought at the store was used up in a month; the vats used to make it were in place for decades. The notion of durability, in fact, is built into the accounting definition of capital. In order for a purchased good to be "capitalized" on the balance sheet, it has to stick around for at least a year.

This reliable old distinction, however, is becoming more subtle. Given the speed with which businesses and product lines change – and, yes, blur – it is clear that, whatever time-span "enduring" used to mean, it is a lot shorter now. Last year's machine tooling is likely to be no more marketable than last year's fashion and as useless as last year's bread. Enduring is also a problematic concept when so much of today's productive capacity is made up of intangible assets. The programmable controls now featured on assembly-line equipment are a good example; they muddy the question of how much of it is enduring and how much evanescent. The hardware is lasting and becoming less valuable than the short-lived and more valuable intangible: software.

Finally, adding connectivity poses its own challenges to the distinction between capital and consumption goods. When the chip in the car remains connected to the computer at the factory, where does the capital good leave off and the consumption good begin?

The point here is that capital goods are more frequently behaving like consumption goods. One implication of this is that any acquisitions should be weighed carefully, with an expectation that obsolescence will begin to set in immediately (i.e. focus on acceleration, not speed). Even more strongly and surprisingly, it means we should actively work to minimize the lifetime of capital goods. In other words, get as much out of them as possible while the getting's good.

The basic advice translates into four axioms about capital in the blurred world.

1. *Use it, do not own it.*

2. *If you do own it, use it up.*

3. *Design to throw away.*

4. *Design to reconfigure.*

# 13

## Business wins, organization kills

Draw a circle in your mind; inside it is your business and outside is your market. Fact: what is outside the circle changes faster than what is inside. Result: most businesses do not keep up and, in the not-so-long run, fall behind. *Lesson from the Future:* any time you have an organization problem, solve it by focusing on the business out there in the marketplace; focusing on the internal problem will only put you further and further behind.

Too many managers confuse their business with their organization. The enterprise you work for is both a business and an organization, but the two are not the same thing. A business is what you do, an organization is how you do it.

This distinction is important because it establishes a cause-and-effect relationship. You cannot possibly know how to do it until you have got an "it" to do. The business comes first and the organization follows. Therefore, by definition, an organization lags behind its business.

How far behind does it lag? Ideally, you want it to follow about a nanosecond behind. That would be a real-time organization, which at this point is an oxymoron. It does not exist yet. What tends to happen is that, in the very beginning of a business's life cycle, there is little or no organization. An entrepreneur wants to escape organization. Then, as the business takes off and grows like crazy, the organization runs like hell to catch up: "We have got to hire people, put in systems and controls and structure." In retrospect, these will be seen as the halcyon days.

At the far end of a life cycle, the business generally has slowed up more than the organization. It takes awhile (too long) for employees to get the message: stop growing your organization; grow your business instead. You do not want the organization tail wagging the business dog. That is a bureaucracy, an inversion of the proper relationship.

A couple of years ago a wave of misplaced organization growth went by the name "learning organization." To be sure, learning and knowledge are tremendously important to business, but you cannot possibly have a learning organization or knowledge management until you have a knowledge business or a learning business.

Our misplaced emphasis is growing knowledge bureaucracies in our companies. We are coining another buzzword, embracing it as the next hot thing, developing all kinds of concepts about it, and letting the organizational focus take off so damn fast that it leaves the business implications in the dust. This is a sure way for the concept to become just a fad and blow up in fairly short order.

This does not have to happen. Instead, first grow your business into a knowledge business. Only then will you truly be able to know what kind of knowledge organization you need to run that business. Smart products, for example, have been doing just that and are worth examining more closely.

Today more computers (microprocessors) are in things like door locks and vending machines than in PCs. Every time we check into a hotel, we get a customized door lock. The next generation of door locks will be interactive, so that when you open the door, they will be connected to systems such as air conditioning, security, and lighting.

As for vending machines, Coca-Cola has 800,000 of them in Japan alone and every one of those vending machines has a chip in it. Ask yourself, what might a vending machine want to know? Some possibilities include the following. How many cans are left? How many times is a button pushed for something that is out of stock? What time of day are purchases highest and lowest? What is the best product mix per machine (not per geographic market)? Is the coin real or counterfeit? What is the optimum internal temperature to keep the drinks properly cold? You do not have to be in the soft-drink business to come up quickly with a number of very direct business concerns that a vending machine might want to know.

Smart products in general might want to know an enormous number of things. Here are some other examples. Is it aligned or misaligned? Available or busy? Charged or discharged? Clean or dirty? Current or expired? Day or night? Early or late? Fast or slow? Firing or misfiring? Fit, misfit, or unfit? Free or pay? Fresh, stale, or spoiled? Full or empty? Hard or soft? High or low? Hot or cold? Important or unimportant? Instantaneous or lagging? Light or dark? Light or heavy? Live or dead? Locked or unlocked? Loud or quiet? Matched or mismatched? On or off? On time or late? Open or closed? Present or absent? Profitable or not? Pure or impure? Pure or blended? Ready or not ready?

You get the point. Spend a lot of time asking what your product wants to know, why, and how it will know it.

What do door locks and vending machines have in common? First, they have "crunching power," tiny microprocessors to log, store, and process information. Second, they are electronically connected. Rather than freestanding, the item is tied into a larger network or system. These two qualities in combination are at the heart of knowledge-driven growth. They are key to transforming the products and services, customers, and markets of every business into a knowledge-based company.

The more embedded "smarts" you have operating in every part of your business, the better off you are. Here is a little exercise. Each time you encounter a smart product, extract the attribute that is at work and ask, how could that principle operate in my business? Build your own checklist.

Here is a simple example. The largest-selling weekly magazine in the USA is *TV Guide*. *TV Guide* is a mature product, the only hope for growth in the future for which is to transform itself into a knowledge-based *TV Guide*. What characteristics would this have? Models that are being developed and sold now are electronically connected, with new listings updated and renewed daily. This means they are upgradable. Features on next-generation guides similarly can be downloaded. Later versions can easily include memory, so that the more you use them, the smarter they get. In time they will learn your viewing habits. Once they do that (while getting better all the time), they are customized. They can be interactive and screen or filter choices for you, suggesting programs you are most likely to want to view. They anticipate: "There is a movie on tonight with your favorite actress, so I will tape it for you."

Extracting the attributes that I have mentioned in this example, knowledge-based products, among other things, have crunching power, are electronically connected, interactive, upgradable, customized, have memory, can learn, filter, and anticipate. Can your company's products and services do these things? What is an interactive pair of socks, a customized mortgage, an upgradable car? Some vehicles, for example, can upgrade their engines and transmissions by using software. How many years will it take before upgradable cars supplant the annual model change and revolutionize the economics of the automotive industry? Probably not more than a decade.

What if your business is in consumables or services? You cannot place a chip on a cornflake, a soap flake, or an intangible. What do you do? You think of your value chain or major business processes and ask what it is these pieces want to know and how these knowledge attributes apply to them. For example, the farm that grows the grain, the factory that makes the cornflakes, the supermarket that sells them, and the consumer who eats them all will become more knowledge intensive. They all will take on the attributes I have described. Precision farming today uses software on the tractor that is connected to the global positioning satellite system. These systems are so sensitive that they can tell where shadows from trees cause lower yields and can adjust the fertilizer and seed mix to take this into account, in real time, when planting.

When every part of your business is knowledge based, knowledge driven, and knowledge intensive, only then is it time to return to your organization and to knowledge management. Only then can you truly avoid growing a knowledge bureaucracy.

In recent years we have focused on efficiency, propping up the declining curve of mature businesses, when we should be using all our smarts and great ideas to get onto the next growth curve. At this moment we need revenue growth more than cost cutting. The more you bring the knowledge focus to your products, services, customers, and markets, the more this very significant concept will have teeth and be real.

Results are outside; inside are only costs. Keep your knowledge focus outside on the marketplace, not inside on the organization.

Many companies, particularly large ones, have a happy fiction called an "internal customer." There is no such thing. The only customer is outside, in the marketplace. Focus your energies there. I leave you with a practical challenge. Each year for the next five years cut in half the number of employees in your company who have no direct customer contact. Too steep? Try cutting it by one-third or even by 10 percent. If you want smart organizations running on knowledge management, this is a good place to begin.

# 14

Running your organization by marketplace rules

This piece is more on the same theme: to make certain that the pace of change inside is as great as that outside, you have to open the borders and boundaries of your organization so that internal activities are run by external marketplace rules. Organizations tend toward bureaucracies. To avoid this fact of life you must embrace the credo that the firm is never firm. What feels blurry and chaotic is likely flexible and adaptive. *Lesson from the Future:* more power to the periphery and do not stop there; cross the border into the outside and run your organization by marketplace rules.

> Freedom has many difficulties and democracy is not per-
> fect, but we have never had to put up a wall to keep our
> people in, to prevent them from leaving us.
>
> John F. Kennedy, Berlin, 1963

Companies put up walls of all kinds, all the time and, by doing so, they restrict the movement of their people, the flow of information between them and the market, and ultimately all opportunities. Only by evolving at the speed of the connected economy and not navel gazing can a company stay in business.

If you hand control to the marketplace, then you will be amazed at how quickly changes will be made. The organizer that your company needs most is the market.

External change takes place exponentially, internal change takes places arithmetically. When a change happens outside, it triggers repeated cascades of economic changes among customers, suppliers, and competitors, each altering the others. When a change is made inside, the ripple effect is lessened by power struggles, politics, culture, status, and organizational inertia. The filters imposed by organizations are so strong that, even if external economics work their way in, it is too late. A gap has opened between where your organization is and where your business needs to be. What is more, the faster things change out there, the greater and more dangerous is the gap between your company's internal and external worlds.

Into this gap pour all those who help organizations change. The more deeply you buy into whatever organizational theory your guru favors, the more thoroughly trapped you are likely to be. Say you adopt the hot organizational principle of the year 2001 and take the minimum two years to change hearts, minds, and systems. When you are done, in 2003, you will have an organization perfectly suited for . . . 2001.

So forget about designing organization. Internal transfer prices, for example, are as inadequate within for-profit corporations as they are between government-run and -owned companies in regulated economies and in those with central planning. Operate your business by the rules of the market and you will enjoy the same advantages that propelled market economies ahead of the planned economies of the world. Hewlett-Packard, for example, has created a two-way auction market for securities whose value depends on how many computers the company sells during a particular feature period. The bid that matches actual sales pays a dividend and, in 19 test runs, the market mechanism proved a better predictor than in-house forecasts.

The bottom line? Because the external pace of change is greater than the internal pace, the only solution is to make sure that your internal organization runs by marketplace rules.

## Open your borders . . .

Despite their competitive analyses, bidding processes, and industry associations, companies suffocate themselves with centrally planned budgets, network fire walls, and packaged communications to employees.

Meanwhile, as you must know by now, electronic connections are bringing efficient markets to every part of the economy. Yet the same design engineer who uses a software agent to compare on-line prices of the latest Kurt Cobain memorial CD gets told by the purchasing department to pay only so much for grommets – or to buy them from a particular supplier.

The Internet and all other electronic connections with outsiders reduce the costs of quickly finding, buying, and getting what you need from people outside the organization. Friction-free capitalism makes internal organization obsolete. The market rules outside, power rules inside.

Ironically, as Peter Drucker pointed out, "Computers have done a great deal of harm by making managers even more inwardly focused. Executives are so enchanted by the internal data the computer generates – and that's all it generates so far, by and large – they have neither the mind nor the time for the outside. Yet results are only on the outside."[1]

Many tried to expand their vision by building "extranets" – separate information systems carefully kept apart from the intranets already in place. They saw only downside risk to blurring the internal fixtures of administrative power with the chaos of efficient markets. Their hearts were in the right place, but not their networks.

*Inter matters more than intra.* Intranets are designed to link internal employees with one another and to grow an organization. Extranets link people across organizations and grow business. The Internet resolves the conflict, linking the smallest and largest players and erasing the boundary between inside and outside. By burrowing through internal silos and the corporate perimeter, the Internet blurs the internal and external, the business and organization. Doing business within your firm may even be riskier than doing business with the outside world. Let's face it: without a culture of risk, an employee will not connect with the guy in the next cube, let alone the customer across the world!

## . . . And let the market in

The fact is, what is happening in the outside world permeates every company. Connectivity attaches everyone to the marketplace. The result is that the "factors of production" companies use to make their stuff – raw materials, plant and equipment, and labor – are increasingly obtained "just in time" in the marketplace, rather than owned "just in case." Remember, Ford once had iron mines and steel factories and, through long-term union contracts, essentially owned its labor force, too. Today, GE auctions off its demand for materials and supplies and Cyrix makes chips in random silicon foundries. Self-employment, as we have noted, is growing faster than any other kind. Support services are bought from outside. Outsourcing legal services is nothing new, but having Kinko's come into your office to set up and operate your mailroom is.

Now you have no idea who the guys at the watercooler really work for. Whoever they are, your company is more efficient because, when you deal with outsiders, you are operating by marketplace laws of supply and demand, which is not the case when your transactions are internal. Internally, costs are blurred, fudged, and buried as overheads. Contract out a part, service, or function and competitive market forces will allow you to gauge such factors as price, time and quality.

This is not about outsourcing as a way to get lean and still keep the walls up. Even if you have no intention of buying outside, you should still look beyond your own borders. You are obliged to look out in the marketplace for a reality check.

Each element of the organization must be competing in an external marketplace, not just supplying internal customers. Your mailroom? Its performance should be better than Kinko's or you should not be running it. Product engineering? Why not outsource to IDEO and other design-for-hire companies? Information systems? Do not even think of custom coding – buy a software package and hire a systems integrator. Factory production? Consider outsourcing from custom manufacturing facilities. Why would any company think that it can run a peripheral cost center better than an outside firm can run that same activity as a full-time business?

Then, make sure that the competencies you keep in-house are competing in the market for what they do. Think of them as separate companies. Here is a practical challenge: Make sure every internal group sells more than 20 to 40 percent of its services in the open market. This means that the internal price will have to be in real currency, not the funny money called "internal transfer price."

If your people cannot sell their services outside, then either the market does not want your people's services (in which case, why do you?) or someone outside is outperforming your people (in which case, why not buy it from them?).

You should scrutinize capital allocation stringently. In principle, each project that is seeking capital should behave like a start-up, competing with all the other great ideas for the attention and backing of venture capitalists. If capital budgeting systems operated this way, then they would perform like local capital markets instead of like political conventions.

Economics, not politics. Business, not organization. Build an ass-kicking culture, not an ass-kissing one. In the world of future wealth, everyone inside an organization is also outside, subject to marketplace forces. That is as it must be.

## Move power to the periphery – and beyond

Industrial technologies are concentrating ones. They thrive on economies of scale and require large supporting organizations. However, organizations turn inward as they grow. Like a balloon when it is inflated, the internal volume increases much more rapidly than does the surface area, so the number of internal workers increases much more rapidly than does the number of those with direct marketplace contact.

As long ago as the 1980s, some corporations identified these problems and tried to cure them by breaking their organization into any number of small business units. The smaller the organizational unit, the thinking went, the closer it would be to market forces. ABB (the Swiss–Swedish industrial giant now organized into more than 1300 units), Corning (a US glass maker), and Thermoelectron (a Waltham, Massachusetts, manufacturer of scientific, medical, and industrial instruments) were among those to steer by this star. In each example, the corporation bought more risk and time will reveal the pay-off.

Information technologies came along just in time to fuel these experiments. By their nature, such technologies are distributive, they do not require large scale, and they bring the outside world in. Now everyone – regardless of rank, location, or time – can have access to the same information. This flattens hierarchy and shifts power to the periphery.

This migration is not about to be stopped by a boundary that is crumbling as we speak. The more the connected infrastructure matures, the more power will migrate beyond the periphery, putting more of a company's decision-making power in non-employees' hands. Already, customers not only dictate Toyota's production schedule but also submit their own list of options which they want the factory to build in. In 1997, Downes and Mui, in *Unleashing the Killer App*, recommended that leaders "outsource to the customer."[2]

Learning to change as fast as the marketplace means that customers are, in effect, designing your organization. When your organization changes as fast as your business, that is as it should be. What seems like the risk of reallocating your resources is really the opportunity to keep pace with the market. What feels like chaos is effective adaptation. The firm is never firm.

## Marketplace rules for human capital

We have not forgotten about the most valuable natural resource: human capital. It has a vital role in helping companies run by marketplace rules. Everyone in your organization can already post their résumé on Monster.com and find out how the market for their skills is doing each day. As Monster.com's chief executive officer Jeff Taylor says "Companies will stop posting most jobs and simply choose from among the résumés in the database."[3] Others will be auctioned off. We argued earlier that a company should allocate capital as though it were a venture capitalist betting on the most worthy risks. It will be the same with human capital.

If you run every other part of your business by marketplace rules, can you still treat your employees as if they had no other options? Of course not – that puts them all at risk. Your organization must offer each person the opportunity to maximize their human capital. You need not offer a fat compensation package yet, but at least a prospectus for human capital growth.

## That is a wrap

What is left for the traditional organization when a company operates like a cost-conscious Hollywood producer, assembling requisite resources as needed from the efficient marketplace? In one sense, a lot less. But what comes as a surprise to most companies is that they gain a lot more in speed and creativity. Allowing ideas and people to flow in and out of their organization is a lot less risky than keeping things secret, controlled, and out of sight of the competition. This understanding lies beneath the vibrant, high-frequency transformation and excitement of the Silicon Valley business culture. It is what John Kao advocates in *Jamming*.[4]

By taking this approach, a company ensures that, even inside the organization, it benefits from efficient market – remember the Hewlett-Packard forecasting example. You are creating an organization in which each element has the incentive to adapt to its own marketplace, unimpeded by the politics and budgeting systems of the traditional bureaucracy. And the churn this creates will accelerate innovation.

Finally, it makes it easier to adapt the whole organization to changing times, because each unit is potentially self-sufficient. Even your most valued talent may move on – with your blessing. The producer does not give the cinematographer severance pay when the movie is wrapped.

The organizations of the twentieth century were built around concentrating technologies. The organizations of the twenty-first century will be built around distributive ones. The Berlin Wall fell in 1989. Organizations are not forever, but the more they let the outside in, the better their chances for survival.

# Part IV

Lessons from the past

# 15

## Mid-life crises in three managers

We all still go through pretty much the same identifiable stages and crises in our lives as people did 20 years ago, yet the work setting in which a lot of this drama plays out has changed enormously. This piece may well have you saying two contradictory things to yourself: "My God, how things have changed!" and at the same time, "You know, a lot of that still rings true." Both reactions afford us lessons from the past that we can apply to the future.

The theory of adult development says that there are natural transitions during adulthood, just as during childhood, and that these are specific to different age ranges. Stable periods or phases, with relative calm and consolidation, last for several years and alternate between shorter stages of transitions between the phases that are briefer, more intense, and generally experienced as times of crises. This still seems true.

Very briefly, the first stage, from 16–18 to 22–24 years,

involves leaving the family and setting out on one's own. Next comes entering into the adult world, during our early to late twenties, which often focuses on finding a vocation and a mate. Starting a family still belongs here, also, although many career-oriented people have been putting this off into their thirties.

The age 30 transition leaves the world of youth behind and moves people into a settling down period, generally combining career growth and raising a family, that lasts until the next crisis, often referred to as "becoming one's own person." This too is succeeded by years of calm, only to move next to a gnawing feeling inside that life is finite, that long-held desires may not be realized, but that there is still time left – even though it is running out – to make one major change. This is often the mid-life transition, somewhere in our forties and it is addressed in the article below.

We describe three vice-presidents who handle their mid-life crisis very differently. The interplay of work and family are the constant context for each, though they play out the crisis and transition in very different ways. As you read their stories, note how "ancient" some of the organization life sounds, yet how recurrent the life dramas still are.

Organization life seems far different today. The Internet, free agentry, home offices, years of a robust economy with full employment – these have all added to a greater sense of personal freedom and choice. The frightened organization man sounds like a relic.

A few short decades ago, staying with the same company was the norm and two or three organization changes in an entire career was about maximum. Today, two or three years with any given company is more the norm and no-one is expected to stay with a company for a decade, let alone an entire working career. Reading a résumé then, one might have said "He has worked for six companies in ten years, what is wrong with him." Now, the more likely comment would be "He has only worked for one company in ten years? What is wrong with him?"

*Lesson from the Future:* life's transitions will always be there; embrace them when they hit and see them as the difficult and sometimes painful windows to personal and career growth that they can be.

"I get the willies when I see closed doors. Even at work, where I am doing so well now, the sight of a closed door is sometimes enough to make me dread that something horrible is happening behind it, something that is going to affect me adversely... I can almost smell the disaster mounting invisibly and flooding out toward me through the frosted panes. My hands may perspire, and my voice may come out strange. I wonder why."

The opening words of Joseph Heller's novel *Something Happened* (Knopf, 1974) are the 43-year-old hero's account of what many people experience in real life, namely, a mid-life crisis. A mid-life crisis is an extreme case of the normal process of mid-life transition.

All lives unfold in steps and stages. For both individuals and organizations, transition points are inevitable and necessary. The mid-life transition is a particularly powerful period of change and is distinguishable from other natural transition periods by the nature of the development task that individuals must perform.

At mid-life a person often gives up old dreams and hopes but realizes new capacities and talents instead. A person may give up youth and recklessness but accept the notion of their own aging and eventual death. Regardless, a taking stock, a reckoning, and a reorientation occur, which can be painful.

Because most of the corporations in our society are run by men in their mid-lives who will undergo or have undergone a transition, we wanted to examine how this phenomenon manifests itself in the context of corporate life. To do so we conducted interviews with more than 50 male executives in several major corporations. In our research we interviewed many women and members of minority groups, but because their work situations are often considerably different from those of white males, we did not include interviews with them in this article.

All people react differently to a period of change. Some work at changing daily and silently and end the transition without knowing that they did any development work. They just know they have changed. Others, like Heller's hero, go through hell before they can say they have changed. Still others avoid the painful task altogether, only to find themselves eventually in another kind of hell – they are older and sadder instead of older and wiser.

We illustrate these three reactions to the mid-life transition with three of the interviews we conducted. The subjects are typical of those we interviewed. They are not psychiatric cases but well paid and successful officers of major corporations who have all been on the fast track.

What follows are Bob, Larry, and Tom's stories about what happened to them between their mid-thirties and mid-forties. After each interview we discuss what we think the nature of the transition was, how the individual coped with it, and how it affected his work life.

We think it important that managers not mistake a transition period for failure or catastrophe. Transitions are "critical" decision periods between progress and stagnation. Not all development, personal or otherwise, is a series of crises. Significant change also occurs in people's lives during periods of general stability. It is during turning points, however – during important transitions – when managers need to view crises the way chinese ideograms define them: not as failures but as dangerous opportunities.

## Bob: "it was a crucible"

Bob works for an organization on the *Fortune* list of major corporations. He is among the top 5 percent of the approximately 50,000 employees in the company and is typical of many of the managers we interviewed. He has been with his company for more than 20 years, spending most of that time as a functional specialist in a variety of positions in corporate headquarters.

People who work with Bob and for him speak about him as one of the most seasoned and responsible people in the corporation: "He is the kind of guy you want on your side when you have to go to the mat." Bob's transition began about the time when, as a successful vice-president with a good reputation inside and outside the organization, he received an offer of a new assignment within the company.

Bob:   An announcement was made that two vice-presidents were switching jobs. This was the first they or anyone had heard of it. Three weeks later it was clear that management was scurrying around looking for a replacement for one of the vice-presidents. Apparently the team above him was making him lose his breakfast in the morning. So they came to me: "Wouldn't it be nice if you took the job?" I said, "No way." So somebody laid a hand on my shoulder and said, "You know, I really would like you to do that." And it was a voice I couldn't say no to. I said, "I think it's wrong for me, but I'll try."

You have to understand. They came to me and said, "Take a job because nobody else wants to take it." And I said, "There's nothing in it for me. I have a better job than the one you're asking me to take and you're asking me to go into an area that other people don't want." But somebody asked me to do something for the company. And I did it.

There was nothing at home that detracted seriously from my performance on the job or that caused me any problems. But it was the wrong job for me and it ended in disaster.

Still, if you asked me and if I knew what I know now, "Would I repeat the performance?" my answer would be yes. Because I was in that position when everything was happening, I got a far greater understanding of what was going on in the corporation than anybody else around today.

My new boss was the only guy I've ever worked for who made me feel uncomfortable about my conceptual abilities. He was so quick on his feet and so broad in his knowledge. He'd ask questions I couldn't even think of. But we had no rapport at all. It could have been a real turn-on and I could have grown with him, but there was no invitation to grow. He treated me as if he was saying, "I want to show you how dumb you are, kid," even though I was a few years older than him.

It was a crucible and it put my career back considerably. I was clearly in turmoil, but I didn't know it was happening. I was not in pain or wondering. But one night, after 15 months, they found me unconscious in my office. Later, the president called me at home and said, "Is it getting too rough for you?" I said, "No, not for me." My boss saw my collapse as a great opportunity for us to part company non-destructively. You know, he didn't want to jeopardize my health and all that bullshit.

After that, they created a lousy job for me that was lower than the one I had. I was a loser. I went through a period of absolute stagnation. I could go to work and sleep for six hours a day. It was such a lousy job – acting as a kind of floating ambassador – you could get a kid to do it. But it looked impressive on paper.

That was the only occasion when I've gone through a bad personal time. I really suffered a loss. I was questioning my competence, my ability: Could I ever do it again? Was it a mistake to begin with? And you've got to work your way out of that yourself. You get no help. No one came with any help at all. Not one query.

A lot of the time I walked around feeling lost. On the job, sometimes I tended to play it safe and wouldn't speak up. You keep your mouth shut.

So you spent about four and a half years falling off the track and living through what you describe as purgatory.

Bob:    I know I'm not a singular case. I can walk through our company dining room and point out five senior vice-presidents who have come within an inch of being fired. One person comes to mind who is probably one of the most well-thought-of senior vice-presidents in the place. At one point he came so close to not making it. During that time we met at a bar on the other side of town and I said, "Hang in there. It can't last. Just stay in there."

You think they're terrific guys. You don't know that somewhere along the line in the past five years they got into a tribe or a subculture that tried to reject them and they made it by the skin of their teeth.

Is it perhaps functional to have a non-job during a period when you're working through a life crisis? At that time your focus was internal and having a non-job gave you the time to resolve those issues. Would you have seen any job as engrossing during that period?

Bob:    I buy it. I've thought about it and I've concluded that I wouldn't have changed anything. It may have been for the best – in retrospect – though it was hell while I was going through it.

Bob vividly describes what he went through and, in response to our question about the mid-life crisis, indicates that something profound happened to him during those years of "being all screwed up." At the end of four and a half years, Bob had a different basis for his self-confidence. By overcoming his own worst self-doubts, he achieved a knowledge of his capabilities that the organization with all its labels could not bestow on him. His new self-confidence came from within rather than from without.

Periods of crisis – during which a transformation often takes place – seem to last for two to four years. An event may lead to a person's rehabilitation back into the mainstream of organizational life. Often the arrival of a new boss or someone who knows the person from his or her earlier career serves as a catalyst to put the person back on track.

The reader might well ask "Can I not finesse this difficult mid-life transformation? Is it not possible to change and grow without experiencing and manifesting extreme difficulties?" In fact, many people pass through mid-life this way and often receive rewards from their organizations. But do they escape unscathed?

The answer to that question is both yes and no. Our next two examples, Larry and Tom, went through the mid-life transition without a crisis. Larry is paying a heavy price for his apparently smooth ride through the transition. Tom confronted the pain directly, did his work, and gained the benefits without a crisis.

## Larry: "I have no other life"

To the world at large, Larry is the ultimate success story. He blends the professional with the company man. He has served in line positions in a diverse set of businesses in a single corporation to which he is ultimately loyal. If a seasoned executive in the company needs the counsel of an even more experienced professional, then Larry is often the person they will speak with. Larry is also a mentor to many of the new generation of fast-track managers in their twenties and early thirties. Ten minutes into the interview, Larry revealed his private world.

Larry: I'm 49, so I've been with the company for 20 years. Before that, in my college years, I thought it was important to do something for people. Then I found out that the Ivy League doesn't have schools of social work. I had a pretty good life, rotating through my assignments here and abroad. I've always had an interesting job; it's always been challenging. I haven't had any personal crises with the company.

I'm an unabashed enthusiast for the place. I've never worked for anyone I really didn't enjoy there. I've never been jammed into one of those two-to-six year stints where you have to work for some son of a bitch you can't stand or you feel isn't interested in you. I feel well acquainted with senior management. I've worked for two of the three top guys for extended periods, which does a lot to give you the feeling that you're part of the enterprise, that you're wanted and cared for. I've always had that feeling and I worry that it's probably impossible to give the same sense to people today.

I'm reasonably good working with people and, in this crazy organization, I'm considered a useful, cohesive force. I have a reasonably broad perspective on what we're doing. So if I have a theme, it's that I do like and believe in the organization.

The theme we hear is "good news." Through two decades, you have enjoyed what you do and every so often you have been pleasantly surprised to find yourself up one more notch with another great assignment. Is that how you see it?

Larry:  Well, my satisfaction with my business life is high, though I feel my personal life is much too submerged by my business and I give myself substantially lower marks outside the company. My family life is at best average. Most of my kicks come from the organization. I get up at 5:30 to jog, hit the train at 7:00, come into work charged up, run my battery right down to zero, and by the time I get home, between 7:00 and 8:00, I'm not ready for anything but a scotch, dinner, a game of ping-pong with my kids, and bed.

I'm fairly athletic, but I don't really have any intellectual or social interests outside the company. My energy is mainly directed toward the company, which my wife resents. I don't know whether my kids resent it, but that's the way it is.

I'd say my wife and I have a mediocre relationship. I accept my marriage as not being very good. I'm afraid there's not much I can do about it. It's not bad enough to leave and what satisfaction I get comes from my kids. I enjoy them and, for the few years left that they'll be around, I want to maintain my home. So I think I see myself pretty clearly. I've made peace with myself and I think I'm much more of a realist than I was earlier when I was in perpetual motion.

When I was younger I worked my ass off and I was a confirmed optimist. I just kept moving, overcoming things by sheer energy and commitment, but with a fair amount of tension and anxiety – which just drove me to more effort, kept me flailing away. That's a costly way to go about doing something and it blots out everything else. You burden yourself, you burn up all your energy with that attitude.

So I wish that 15 or so years ago I'd been more mature. I might have oriented my outside life better and might have had a chance at the policy board – which is a long shot now unless the chief decides that they ought to have an old man there.

You are 49. What are your thoughts about the future?

Larry: I don't really think about the future. I have no other life. I'm locked into this. And really, I'm quite unhappy and unsatisfied, so the whole future seems screwed up. But I'm running from that. A week from tomorrow I catch a plane to Argentina, then to Brazil, then to Mexico. I'll have a good time, along with anxiety.

## Larry's transformation

By his own admission, Larry is a success only in the eyes of others. Because he has never ceased to fulfill strictly organizational criteria for success, the company continues to reward him. The bitter irony is that the rewards he receives from work have become less and less meaningful to his sense of success.

If in response to the questions of an inner voice, a person creates a closer and better fit between their needs and their career during their mid-life decade, then they satisfy their questioning and continue their work as a labor of love. If, on the other hand, the inner questioning does not lead a person to change during this period, the issues and emotions they suppress may instead lead to an internal schism. By refusing to balance inner with outer needs, family with work, a person sacrifices integrity.

The most critical and poignant aspect of the struggle to grow is the attempt to balance family and work. During their apprenticeships, people tend to work excessively long hours and to use work as a way to avoid intimacy at home. Forty year olds, however, generally no longer have to work that hard. The choice is theirs alone – either to let go of work as a defense against intimacy and achieve a better balance between the two or else to avoid this major task, as Larry did and slip irretrievably back into domination by old themes.

## Tom: "I'm a known quantity"

Tom is also a vice-president in a large corporation. He has always had line positions, first as a functional specialist, then as a general manager in larger profit centers. Tom has reached the position of a one-star general in his company and is likely to stay there. At this station he leads a balanced personal and work life. He does not let this work dominate his life to the extent Bob or Larry do. Yet one gets the feeling that it cannot quite all be as fine as he makes it sound. Even for Tom there is no free lunch, although it is harder to see the price tag.

Tom:   I've been with the company for almost 20 years, most of the time in the same group. I'm a department head now. I haven't spent any time overseas, which I would love to. I got divorced ten years ago when my kids were still fairly young. I told my boss that, everything else being equal, I would prefer to stay here until they went away to college. I think I passed up a couple of good opportunities, but I knew that was the risk I ran. So I hope that in the next couple of years, if the right opportunity comes along – like running a foreign operation – that I could do that for four or five years.

I got married about 20 years ago and I've lived since then in the country, about 50 miles north of here. During my whole career I've commuted back and forth. My ex-wife and I live five miles apart, so the kids are very close by; they are an important part of my life. I see a great deal of them.

Outside the company, I'm mainly interested in outdoor sports. I love fishing and camping and hiking and hunting; I love golf and tennis.

The view you take of your job as well as your personal world is intriguing. Some people feel they have burned their bridges and do not have options, while you seem to feel that you have got practically a whole lifetime ahead of you. What helped you to look at your life this way?

Tom:   I am a very positive individual. The job is exciting and I've never felt stymied. Still, I could have been in a more responsible job with a bigger title if I had not wanted to stay here until my kids grew up. But that was a decision I made.

Another thing is, whom do I have to impress? I've been in the company for 20 years and everybody knows who the hell I am. I'm a known quantity.

My work is not the overriding part of my life. On a scale

of 100, the company would be well below 50. But that doesn't mean I don't work my ass off, because I do. Other things are just more important to me than the company. I look around and see some of the people I call "gray people." Christ, they can't even walk across the street and have a drink without wanting to talk business. I think, "It must be sad." I see people going home on the train and I wonder, "God, what are they going home to?" Half of them down three drinks and fall asleep on the train and get up the next morning and do the same thing all over again.

The goddamn meeting I went to yesterday was a disaster. A whole bunch of gray people. They all looked like under-takers – 200 of them. There wasn't a joke, there wasn't a smile, there wasn't a light line in the whole presentation. I almost went to sleep. They were like automatons. Turn them on, line them up, put them on stage. They are a bunch of gray people talking about business. I think the company encourages that side of them and it's too bad, because there are a lot of damn good people here.

Some of them are forever chasing that next place they want to be, the next $40,000, the next promotion and they are not enjoying anything about getting there. That has not happened to me and I don't want it to happen to anybody who works for me. It doesn't impress me at all if somebody stays at work until 8 p.m. I would say, "There's something wrong; we're not organized. Let's work hard and get the work out, but boy, let's kid around and have some fun too."

## The importance of balance

All three men accepted new assignments with more questions than they had asked when they were young and they more frequently asked themselves whether they really wanted to do such assign-ments. For Bob and Tom, the illusion of safety finally died, but for Larry the inevitable was still something to avoid.

From interviews with dozens of people like Bob, Larry, and Tom we have come to believe that the prize for a successful mid-life transition is a liberation from strict adherence to the remaining codes and regulations imposed by the people who formed us – our parents and our bosses, our partners, and our colleagues. Bob and Tom seem to have earned their prizes, while Larry backed away from even trying for his.

As Tom's case shows, a wife and children often participate, willingly or not, in defining the balance between home and work. The career-focused man, like Larry, is usually a mixed blessing to other family members. They are proud of him and benefit from the rewards that he brings, but they also want him to share more of their lives and vice versa.

When work is unrewarding, as it was for Bob in his non-job, the person will probably be more receptive to support from home than at any other time. Sympathy from those at work may be less therapeutic than support from home, which can benefit the individual, their family, and the organization.

People who are going through what has come to be called the mid-life crisis are generally neither unstable nor burned out. Rather than seeing them as exemplifying the Peter principle, managers would make sounder career and promotional decisions if they saw the struggle as evidence that these people had not yet reached their full potential.

The mid-life transition engages people in a process of reorientation and reintegration that equips them for further and continued advancement, which they would not experience without this upheaval. It is now several years since we first interviewed these three men; each is still with his same company and doing well in his job.

# 16

---

# Are corporate cultures still relevant?

Cultures are the secular souls of companies. Managers believe this with impressive tenacity despite the lack of results that such beliefs have brought to their companies' performance. Corporate cultures are real but, after all the hoopla, have they really mattered?

My conclusion is that the social awareness about corporate culture has been greater than the economic effect. Despite the fact that the thing exists and has a powerful impact on the way work is done in a company, it would be difficult to point to many substantial and enduring changes that have resulted from all the attention. Instead, I would say that workplaces with terrific cultures have them because of the healthy way the people focus on their business, not the way they focus on their culture.

Many companies invest a great deal of time, energy, and money "transforming" their cultures. However, after these projects end and their attention turns elsewhere, most companies seem hardly changed at all. And yet these same people and companies still continue to affirm the importance of their corporate cultures.

Part of the reason the culture focus has not produced better results is because the notion was reified, the abstraction was made into a thing. Managers tried to make it objective and concrete. Various statements of values and beliefs, produced by chief executive officers and their minions, were found in great variety, embedded in lucite cubes on desktops, framed on office walls, and sealed in plastic cards for the wallet. Most were enshrined, then forgotten. They were artifacts, not the culture.

The main reason corporate culture efforts did not produce better results is that they focused almost exclusively on the organization culture when they should have focused on the business culture. A business is the application of resources in order to create products and services that meet market needs, in relation to competitors. An organization is the way in which those resources get administered. Organization is the means of accomplishing businesses' ends. Most culture work has been about how to manage, not about how to compete. It should be the opposite. *Lesson from the Future:* the best corporate cultures are the ones that are built around the purpose of the enterprise rather than around the management of the organization. Solve your organization problems by creating business opportunities rather than by focusing on organization cultures *per se.*

An approach I have found very useful relies on constructing a simple matrix for assessing the cultural risk. When a business goes to implement its strategy, it chooses a number of specific actions. Steps that are contrary to the cultural reality will encounter resistance. Actions more compatible with the daily culture will be more readily accepted. In addition, while each of a series of steps is aimed at implementing the strategy, some are more important than others. The degree of cultural risk, therefore, depends on the answers to two important questions: How important is each action to the success of the strategy? and How compatible is each action with the daily culture? These two questions, each ranked high/medium/low, can then be arrayed on a 3 × 3 matrix as shown in Figure 16.1.

Notice that the segment on the lower left will contain actions or

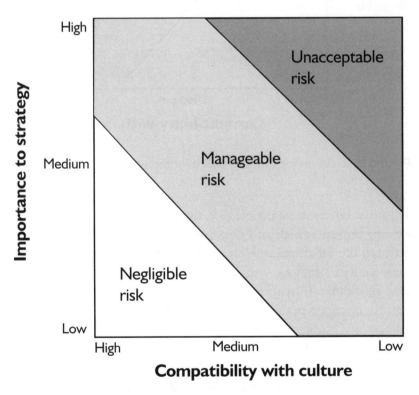

**Figure 16.1** Assessing cultural risk.

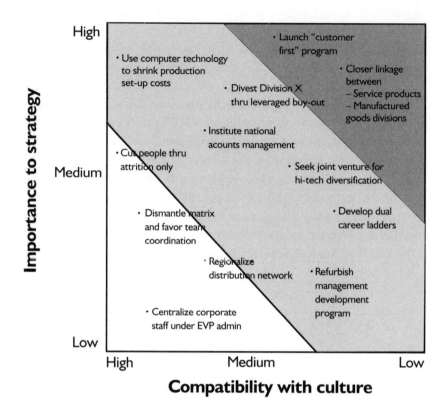

**Figure 16.2** Assessing cultural risk in company X.

steps that represent negligible risk, since their compatibility with the existing culture is high and they are not crucial to the strategy anyway. On the other end, the far upper right-hand area will highlight those activities that are critical to strategy but that fly in the face of existing culture. If neither the strategy nor the culture change, these represent unacceptable risks. In the middle area will fall other aspects of strategy that we may label manageable risk, insofar as they are neither fatal nor benign and, if something is done about them, the risk can be diminished. Obviously, the boundaries separating negligible, manageable, and unacceptable risk are not fixed and depend on judgement.

The next step is to take the specific actions called for in implementing the strategy and place them in what you consider to be their appropriate position on the grid. Figure 16.2 is an example of what this might look like for one company.

The items listed in the grid are steps the company will be taking to implement its strategic plan. Remember, these have been placed according to an assessment of their relative importance for achieving the strategy and their relative compatibility with that company's culture. You will see, for example, the two items – the Customer First program and the closer linkage between service products and manufactured goods divisions – will be the two implementation steps that are simultaneously the most critical and the most risky because they are so countercultural.

Judging by experience, when you work with a group of managers it is relatively easy to gain agreement about the placement of items in this grid. Moreover, it is not necessary to have a complete list in order to use this approach. Items can be added at any time. The point is that it helps to identify those proposed steps where the major dangers and unacceptable risks lie.

The placement of items can be done by yourself, in workshops with colleagues or a facilitator, or in any number of other groupings. Working alone, you may find it will take you about five minutes. After doing this alone, however, I suggest that deciding where the items belong on the chart is better accomplished through discussion than by just taking an average score of all those who fill it in. The chart is a framework for identifying where the problems lie and it is also an excellent vehicle for beginning discussions about how to solve those problems.

In assessing the importance of each item to the final success of a strategy, it is useful to keep in mind several key guidelines. One is to find out what specific behavior the action is designed to encourage. Related to this is determining how this behavior is linked to critical success factors. For example, what specific customer needs or requirements is the behavior intended to satisfy? What competitive advantage will be gained in the marketplace? What impact will such behavior have on costs? What impact will this behavior have on external factors such as government, regulatory agencies, the financial community, public opinion, prospective employees?

It is critical to know the beliefs that guide you and the cultural risk matrix offers a way to make those beliefs explicit. But a more difficult and controversial issue remains – whether or not to judge the worthiness of a belief. My position is that such judgements are the responsibility of corporate leadership. It is of the utmost importance, however, for the analyst or manager to point out the pluses and minuses of the guiding beliefs in relation to the corporation's strategic objectives.

An example from a client will help make the distinction clear. This company is emerging from a regulated environment where managers appreciate the need to strengthen the company's marketing capabilities, one way they described their belief about marketing was "Use marketing as a tool for differentiating customers and determining how we can profitably serve them." What these words express is that marketing is simply one of several tools in their kit. Since the company never had to be very customer focused before, this narrow view of marketing was not unexpected. What had to be made explicit is that truly customer-oriented companies regard marketing not as a tool, but as a way of life. It is something you are, not something you use. To keep the company mindful of the difference, we used the phrase, "marketing: tool or Tao?" Once we pointed this out, management could see that they were taking a narrow market research orientation and using it as a way to focus on more product development rather than on customer service.

In this case the company's belief also reflected how it approached this activity from its own needs rather than from the customers' needs. It had started with itself and was bringing marketing tools to its business activities. Its people were not living by a basic rule of marketing, which is to start with the customer. Good alternatives might have been "We place the customer first, delivering the best value in services to more people" or "Provide the services customers need, where and when they want them."

The discipline and simplicity of the cultural risk matrix forces planners and managers to think hard about the relationship between a business plan and the organization designed to carry out that plan. The method also demonstrates a way that cultural risk analysis can be systematized, so that managers can see clearly what effect their proposed actions are likely to have. Many in management fail to appreciate how cultural risk can derail even the most powerful strategies.

# 17

## Organization that won't go away

While methods of management and organization have changed enormously during the information economy, a few basic elements from decades past still survive. We seldom hear of line and staff or centralized and decentralized any more, for example, but we do still understand that organizations have structures and that the groupings are often around such perennial pieces as divisions and strategic business units. One notion that never worked satisfactorily yet never disappeared is the matrix form of organization. (The day before I wrote this, I actually received a royalty check for my book *Matrix*, first published in 1978.)

Why should an unsatisfactory form of organization continue for so long, and amidst such profound change in business? The answer is because the problem that needed solving is still with us. Here is the issue. There are only a limited number of ways to organize, really four: by products, functions, geography, or markets. Whichever way you choose, you do not get the benefits of the other ways. Imagine a big sphere that you want to divide up into its most logical parts and you have four knives to use but can only use them one at a time. If your first cut is into products, then you can stack basic functions within product divisions or geography within functions, and so on. But any choice is sequential, not simultaneous.

A matrix was meant to be a way to organize simultaneously around more than one dimension: a function × product matrix or a product × market matrix. The excerpt below tells you the essentials of its form in business and elsewhere.

The amazing thing is that many companies still use it. It seems that we still search for a holy grail for organizing ourselves some impossible "best" way. A matrix is like an old suit of clothes; we do not love it any more, but it is familiar so we keep on wearing it and occasionally wonder why.

Now, decades later, I see a glimmer, the emergence of what might be a better way. There are some activities that companies need to do, but it is not the business they are in: information technology, purchasing, advertising, and so on. They have increasingly been outsourcing such activities to firms whose sole purpose is to be best in the world at providing these needs. As companies outsourced, they created a matrix of firms at the level of economy, outside rather than within the firm. There is great wisdom in this approach. Matrix works better and more naturally between rather than within firms. *Lesson from the Future:* decide what part of your organization are absolutely essential. Outsource everything else. Ally yourself with people who do the activity as their full-time business passion rather than saddling yourself with internal staff who never test their skills in the external marketplace.

Matrix management and organization are spreading in the USA and, to a lesser extent, in other countries. The list of well-known firms that are involved is becoming long and impressive. Take, for example, a company that had 1977 annual sales of $14 billion and employed around 400,000 people in scores of diverse businesses – General Electric (GE). For decades, despite the diversity of businesses, GE used one basic structure throughout its organization: one general manager and five functional managers.

In recent years some of its groups, divisions, and departments have adopted the matrix. The logic is that one must organize to meet the particular needs of each business and, if different business have different needs, then one organization design for all is bound to be inadequate. The matrix is appearing as a fundamental alternative. In a projection of GE's organization over the next ten years, its September 1976 Organization Planning Bulleting stated that

We've highlighted matrix organization... not because it's a bandwagon that we want you all to jump on, but rather that it's a complex, difficult, and sometimes frustrating form of organization to live with. It's also, however, a bellwether of things to come. But, when implemented well, it does offer much of the best of both worlds. And all of us are going to have to learn how to utilize organization to prepare managers to increasingly deal with high levels of complexity and ambiguity in situations where they have to get results from people and components *not* under their direct control. . . . Successful experience in operating under a matrix constitutes better preparation for an individual to run a huge diversified institution like General Electric – where so many complex, conflicting interests must be balanced – than the product and functional modes which have been our hallmark over the past twenty years.

This expresses our own sentiments very well. A few years ago when we would ask a group of diverse executives if their organizations used a matrix only a scattering of hands would appear. Such a question today usually draws a response from well over half of the class. On further questioning it also becomes clear that not all of those responding have a very clear or consistent idea of what they mean by matrix and a fair number will have reacted very negatively to their initial experience with a matrix. So the matrix approach is being tried in more and more organizations, not because of but in spite of limited understanding and mixed reactions.

## What is a matrix?

The term matrix grew up in the US aerospace industry. It probably seemed like a fitting term for mathematically trained engineers in that industry to apply to the gridlike structure that was evolving from its project management origins during the 1950s. Regardless of its origin, it has now become the accepted term in both business and academic circles. But how can we best define it? We believe that the most useful definition is based on the feature of a matrix organization that most clearly distinguishes it from conventional organizations. That is its abandonment of the age-old precept of "one man–one boss" or a single chain of command in favor of a "two-boss" or multiple command system. So we define matrix as any organization that employs a multiple command system that includes not only a *multiple command structure* but also related support mechanisms and an associated organizational culture and behavior pattern. Moving to a matrix organization, as we define it, is a truly significant organizational step. It is distinctly not just another minor management technique or a passing fad. For those business organizations who need a matrix and use it fully, it represents a sharp break with earlier business organization forms. To borrow a biological analogy, matrix represents a new species of business organization, not merely a variant of an existing type. However, is it truly new when we consider the full range of human institutions? We need to put the matrix into perspective.

## Organizational choice

Business organizations have evolved since the start of the industrial revolution as "one-boss" unitary command structures. This is so close to being a universal pattern that managers have been unaware until recently that any choice existed in this matter. Just the mention of the two-boss idea made many managers distinctly uncomfortable. It seemed to them like a violation of natural law, like rewriting the tablets from Mount Sinai. But in even the most traditional businesses, the one-boss rule is often strained. We have often heard such statements as

Somewhere we've got an organization chart that tells you who my boss is, and there's a dotted line going the other way, but I really couldn't say which is which. They're both my bosses, and I doubt if either of them could tell you which is the real one.

Officially, I'm supposed to report to corporate staff, but you know for all practical purposes my real boss is our plant manager.

They say it isn't so, but I know that it is. Sometimes I feel that I've got three or four bosses.

More and more managers feels as if they report to two-bosses regardless of the unitary organization chart. Many who do and most who do not, however, see something messy and troublesome in the notion; as the quotes above suggest, it smacks of indecision and confusion. So many managers find themselves practicing in reality what they reject in theory. Some of these managers are going further to recognize that there is more than one theory, more than one model; that there is an organizational choice. Our ideas about how to organize in business derive from other institutions such as the military, religion, government, and the family. Although the tasks performed in each vary widely, all of them create organizations that distribute power to carry out their purpose. The distribution of power may begin through one or through many sources and this distinction creates two basic organization designs that we will simplify by calling them the one-boss model and the two-boss model.

## One-boss models

The military, the church, and the monarchy are all institutions that believe in and maintain pyramid-like structures whose plumbline is the unity of command. It took nothing less than the convulsions of the Protestant Reformation to create an alternative to the singular hierarchy of the Catholic Church. Despite the pluralism in religious thought and organization, however, business still adopted the unitary belief: thou shalt have but one boss above thee. To create the separation of powers inherent in the British and particularly the American forms of government, we experienced the beheading of a king and revolt of the colonies. And these changes took decades if not centuries to unfold. Why, then, should business institutions be any more amenable to fundamental change in the distribution of power within their organizations than religions and governments have been to the same process within theirs?

Indeed, military organization provided the most important model for early business structures and the scalar principles (power increases as you ascend in a hierarchy, superiors coordinate their subordinates' efforts) and notions of line and staff are still very much alive in both military and industrial complexes. Yet, the ironic fact is that it is at the interface between military and industrial organization, in the aerospace industry, that we today most frequently find matrix organizations. The military, in its need to have a single liaison with any one project in industry, are responsible for prompting a second managerial line and, hence, a pluralist model of managing.

## Two-boss models

While the one-boss model accepts the greater authority of those higher in the hierarchy as a given, the two-boss or multiple-boss model does not relinquish the subordinate's autonomy quite so easily. Hierarchy of power and status is not denied, but it is made plural. The best known examples of this model are found in our families and in our government.

Managers who feel or would feel uncomfortable in a two-boss relationship might do well to remember that we each had both a mother and a father. As children, we were responsible to both of them, both had authority over us and, oedipal problems notwithstanding, the arrangement was basically comfortable. Parent–child conflicts are rarely due to the existence of a second parent; in fact, one parent often eases difficulties the child experiences with the other parent. As adults, most people are still able to negotiate their relationships with both parents and not feel uncomfortable about the duality.

Despite the significant differences between having two parents and having two bosses, nevertheless there are common elements in both situations: parents and bosses both occupy superior positions in their hierarchies and both must share their authority and status over a common subordinate(s). From the child's perspective, when resistance develops it is likely to be over the first element – the drive for independence and away from subordinate status. For the subordinate adult manager, however, resistance is caused by the second element – multiple masters.

To move to another model, relations between nation states have long been handled as a balance of power or what economists call an oligopoly. In an oligopoly, members agree to play by rules which will limit the distribution of wealth to only a few, giving up the goal of gaining complete control in exchange for a guarantee that they will never be excluded from having significant control. Oligopoly among firms is an economic counterpart to a balance of power between nations. Nation states have achieved long periods of peace by such rules, as firms have achieved long periods of prosperity by the same principles applied to economic activities. The balance of power concept, however, has had greater acceptance between nations than within nations. However, the American form of government, among others, is an exception.

The separation of legislative, executive, and judicial powers in the government is a three-boss model. It is intended as a safeguard of individuals' liberty in the face of a government's need to maintain order. The tension between these simultaneous needs of independence and authority can be translated into terms that affect business organizations as well. Business organizations need to divide labor into specialized tasks and to coordinate these tasks for the good of the total corporation. The freedom that comes from decentralized organization must be balanced with the integration and control of centralized forms, much as in the forms of government.

Americans in business are traditionally suspicious of the long arm of government and generally regard its methods of organization as inefficient bureaucratic nightmares. That government's reliance on a balance of power model could have useful counterparts in the organization of business enterprise usually provokes the comment "What profit did the government ever make?" The point is well taken, but so is the rebuttal: business has used the military for its model and what profit has the military made? Different institutions can and do use the same model for different purposes.

The important point is that the spectrum of human institutions offer us choice in regard to organizational models. Business firms are now opening up this question and considerable number are moving from the one-boss to the two-boss or multiple-boss model.

# Part V

Lessons from the future

# 18

## The bio-economy

The next economy is gestating right now. What will it be about? The bets have already been placed and the results are in: biotechnology will be the next great wave after information technologies. It will begin in areas like pharmaceuticals and agriculture and, ultimately, spread throughout every economic sector, just as computers did before. This piece, written for *Time* magazine, gives you a feel for what this next economy — the true economy of most of the twenty-first century — will be like. *Lesson from the Future:* biotechnology today is where computer technology was in the 1960s. Its impact will be enormous and, unless you plan to retire within the next decade, start to understand it now.

We did not realize we were no longer living in an industrial economy for about 20 years, from the early 1950s to the early 1970s. When we finally figured out the old economy had exited, we did not know what to call the new one. Post-industrial? Service? Shopping and gathering? Information won the title.

Get ready for *déjà vu* all over again. Like everything else, all economies have beginnings and endings and we can already see the end of this one a few decades hence. Economies end not because they peter out but because a challenger supplants them. That is what will happen around a quarter-century for now.

Hunting-and-gathering economies ruled for hundreds of thousands of years before they were overshadowed by agrarian economies, which ruled for about 10,000 years. Next came the industrial ones. The first began in Britain in the 1760s and the first to finish started unwinding in the USA in the early 1950s. We are halfway through the information economy and, from start to finish, it will last 75 to 80 years, ending in the late 2020s. Then get ready for the next one: the bio-economy.

Life cycles for people and plants, for businesses, industries economies, and entire civilizations have four distinct quarters: gestation, growth, maturity, and decline. The Internet is the main even of the information economy's mature quarter, the last phase of it being marked by the widespread use of cheap chips and wireless technology that will let everything connect to everything else. Life cycles overlap. So the information economy will mature in the years ahead as the bio-economy completes its gestation and finally takes off into its growth quarter during the 2020s.

The bio-economy opened for business in 1953, when Francis Crick and James Watson identified the double-helix structure of DNA. The bio-economy has been in its first quarter ever since and completion and publication of the decoded human genome marks the end of this gestation period.

We are heading into the second or growth quarter, when hot new industries appear, much as semiconductors and software did in the second quarter of the information economy. Thus, biotechnology will pave the way for the bio-economy era. During the next two decades, organic biotechnology will overlap with inorganic silicon infotechnology and inorganic composite materials and nanotechnologies.

During the overlap of infotechnology and biotechnology, we will be digitizing many biological processes. Up until now, four kinds of information have dominated: numbers, words, sounds, and images. But information comes in many other forms, such as smell taste, touch, imagination, and intuition. The problem is that our technologies for smell taste, and other new information forms are not yet developed enough to make them commercially viable. By the 2020s, they will be.

Smell, for example, perhaps the most primal of senses, is being digitized the way sight and sound have been. The basics of what makes a smell can be captured molecularly and expressed digitally on a chip at a reasonable price. Companies like DigiScents of Oakland, California and Ambryx of La Jolla, California, have already developed digital odors. Cyrano Sciences of Pasadena, California, is developing medical-diagnostics technology that can "smell" diseases.

Imagine sending a greeting card that incorporates the smell of flowers with a written and graphic message. By the 2020s, digital movies will have their own distinctive smell prints. (You can watch Haley Joel Osment in a remake of *The Beach* and smell the coconut oil!) Why stop there? How does a bank smell and how does Chase smell different from Citigroup? How about retailers? This is only a tiny example of what will come.

More fundamentally, the first four industries to be infused by the bio-economy era will be pharmaceuticals, health care, agriculture, and food.

Best known are the dozens of bio-engineered drugs already on the market. Most of these save lives by treating existing problems. One of the biggest shifts for biotechnology in the decades to come then will be the way it transforms the health care paradigm from treatment to prediction and prevention. Health care today is really sick care. The sick care business model made money by filling hospital beds. Currently, we are in the managed care model. It is transitional, lasting one to two decades. Here, you make money by emptying beds. In the bio-economy, health care will work on a preventive model, making money by helping people avoid having to enter a hospital in the first place.

Basic needs are met in every economy by using the latest technologies available. In the bio-economy of the 2020s, the farm will be a super-bio-engineered place with multimillion-dollar manufacturing plants instead of fields.

Today bio-engineered milk, meat, and produce are already on our supermarket shelves. Numerous varieties of corn are biogenetically altered – albeit not without challenge. One study showed that pollen from some strains of altered corn killed the larva of the monarch butterfly. Fears of Frankenfoods have caused enough of a furor to disrupt Monsanto's life sciences strategy and help topple its chief executive officer. Such incidents will certainly multiply.

Beyond 2025, when we move into the mature bio-economy the effects and applications of biotechnology will spread into sectors seemingly unrelated to biology. In the 1950s and 1960s it was difficult to comprehend that computers would change every industry – from manufacturing to hotels to insurance – just as it is now tough to see how biotechnology will alter non-biological businesses. By the third quarter of the next economy, somewhere in the mid-century, bio-applications will seep into many of the nooks and crannies of our non-biological lives.

Problems will spread as much as benefits do. Each era produces its own dark side. The industrial era was accompanied by pollution and environmental degradation. The major problem of the information age is privacy. In the bio-economy, the issue will be ethics. Cloning, bio-engineered foods, eugenics, genetic patenting, and certainty about inherited diseases are just a few of the many developments that are already creating a storm. And the storm will intensify in the USA.

All this will make baby boomers a unique generation. They will be the first in history to span three distinct economies. Born at the end of the industrial period, they will spend their entire careers in the information age and will end their days watching their grand-children negotiate the bio-economy.

Generation Xers, born after 1964, will be different. During their working years, they will experience two major economic shifts: first, from the crunching to the connecting halves of this information economy and, second, from a microwave-based connected universe to the cell-based world of biologic and bionomics. Those of you in generation Y may have to go through three!

However long you will spend in it, the bio-economy is the next one to be born and, of all economies past, present, and future, it will exert an impact that will make the info-economy look like the runt of the litter.

# 19

---

# Bottoms up: here's to
# the next economy

In the future bio-economy economic value will be created at the molecular level. The bridge between computer code (based on 0 and 1) and genetic code (based on C, G, A, and T) will lead to the blurring between organic and inorganic life. Code is code. And the economy, like life, will build from the bottom up. *Lesson from the Future:* ask "what is the molecular level in my business and how can it deliver value?"

There is an old story of two morons who wanted to build a house, but were not sure if they should build it from the bottom up or from the top down. They started anyway. A few weeks later a construction crew started building another home across the street. One of the morons went over to them and said, "Excuse me, but when you build a home do you build it from the bottom up or from the top down?" The builders looked at him and said, "What are you a moron? You build from the bottom up, of course!" The moron turned to his companion and shouted, "Hey Joe, tear it down. We have to start over."

Biology operates at four distinct levels: DNA, organisms, species, and ecologies. Life starts at the tiny level and builds up. In other words, ecology is derivative of molecules, not vice versa, unless you are a creationist.

The design principle of building from the bottom up operates in economics as well as biology. All venture capital investments in biotechnologies are focused on the tiny end of this spectrum. This means that, in the bio-economy of the future, economic value will probably be created at the molecular level. So far, there have been two such waves.

The first wave of venture capital into biotechnology was dominated by recombinant DNA. The economic model was very similar to big pharma's, involving large sums of money, big mixing vats, regulations and trails, long lead times, big risks, and making replacement drugs for targets whose molecular structure was poorly understood. This produced products like insulin replacement, interferon, and human growth hormone and companies like Genentech, Cetus, and Chiron. When problems arose, the money line shrivelled and most start-ups sold out to better-capitalized pharmaceutical giants.

The new wave operates with a different economic model. Companies and research are based on genomics, an emerging offshoot of biotechnology that studies complete information codes in the molecules of different species. While the techniques are akin to molecular biology and genetic engineering, the tools that it uses are closer cousins to the information technology world of computers.

This is often called bio-informatics and the firms have more in common with information technology start-ups than they have with big pharma.

Drug companies are marketing experts who start with a drug that needs to go through clinical trails and has to be regulated. In contrast genomics starts at the front end with the computing technologies and tools to crack the information code of a species. Only once it understands the molecular structure of a target does it move towards identifying potential treatments and solutions.

Successful decoding of the entire genome of a yeast, worm, and fruit fly have been important steps to the decoding of the human genome. Because code is code and because we share approximately 40 percent of our genome with the fruit fly, they are model systems for human biology. (We share approximately 98.6% of our genome with chimpanzees, so could it be that what makes us truly human lies in that tiny 1.4% difference?) The major event in this second wave has been the initial completion of sequencing of the human genome, announced in June 2000.

With sequencing complete, we can now expect an applications race, major venture capital investments, and rapid growth in companies employing genomics. Initially this will be in health care, focusing on discovery of new proteins, drug targets, and diagnostic markets. Other health care applications will emphasize early detection, screening, and prevention. Colon cancer, for example, is largely curable, but because the current method – colonoscopy – is so inconvenient and expensive, it often is not caught until it is too late. Using genomics, Exact Labs, in Maynard, Massachusetts, is developing a test using stool samples. These are fast, cheap, and do not require regulation.

Another early application will be in pharmacogenomics, studying genetic variations in order to determine risk efficacy. Not all people who smoke, for example, develop smoking-related cancers and pharmacogenomics can develop tests to identify those most at risk. Companies who are pioneering this approach, such as Glaxo Wellcome, foresee the day when all drugs will be mass customized to the genome of specific individuals.

The second wave will likely build much faster than the first. Its business model is geared to revenue streams and payback within a year or two. It begins with code, uses bio-informatics liberally, and finesses trials and regulatory issues. It will spread more quickly to other sectors, such as agribusiness and food processing, chemicals, energy, and environment. It will find applications in materials science, sensors, robotics, nanotechnology, and other new inorganic industries. It will also involve related industries that service these new ones as diverse as computing, mutual funds, law firms, and over-the-counter home health care tests and appliances.

Like automobiles in the industrial era, the importance of computers far transcends their industry and is essential for all economic activity today. Biotechnology and its offshoot, genomics, is likely to play this same role in the future bio-economy. It will probably become an enormous growth industry during this decade and then go on to applications and usage far beyond the industry itself.

When computers began to connect with one another, there was a lot of talk about blending computer and telecommunications industries (called C&C). At the time, there was a lot of ink explaining why IBM and AT&T were destined to be direct competitors in their core businesses. This never happened, of course. The same misinterpretation is now forming around biotechnology. As its importance, applications, and reach grow, bringing more and more sectors under its influence, there is a tendency to see health care, pharmaceuticals, medicine, chemicals, agribusiness, and a handful more merging into one gigantic "life science" sector. That is not going to happen. These industries will all use biotechnology. In every case it will impact on their basic business model and it will result in significant alliances and coevolution across these vertical sectors. But they will remain distinct.

The driving force will be at the most basic, molecular level. As Dr. Noubar Afeyan put it in a MIT lecture (25 September 2000) "molecular biology is the study of nature's operating system and genomics is the (open) source code of life." In this analogy, DNA is nature's microprocessor. Dr Afeyan, a leader in the commercialization of molecular biology, was chief business officer of Celera

Genomics during its two-year climb (1998–1999) from $500 million to $12 billion market value.

The technologies of both biology and computers work on very similar information codes. Computers, the foundation for the information economy, work on a two-letter code of 0 and 1. DNA, the foundation of all organic life, works on a four-letter information code (C, G, A and T). In each case, moreover, the information scales up through successive layers, over micromoments or millennia, until you have enterprises and organisms, industries and species, economies and ecosystems. The world is built on code from the bottom up and so are the economies that populate it. Still, in its essential and elemental form, code is code. Conceptually, it can be treated interchangably and work is now under way to make this concept practical.

One level above code, where code is processed, a fundamental obstacle is looming. At the most basic level, biology is able to cram all its information inside the nucleus of every cell. Silicon, however, has a fundamental limitation problem. The well-known Moore's law states that the number of circuits on a silicon chip, that is the processing power of the computer, will double every 18 months with no increase in price or, alternatively, that in the same time period the same computing power will cost half as much. While literally a guideline rather than a law, this astounding rule has held true since Gordon Moore posited it in 1965, three years before he co-founded Intel.

The problem is that there are real physical limits to how much computing power can get crammed onto a chip. At the current rate, over 1 billion transistors will be crammed on before 2015. Tolerances are widely expected to reach their absolute limits before 2020 and are now rapidly approaching the 0.1 micron level, where insulating layers are only a few atoms deep. A fundamentally new basis for computing will be necessary but, as yet, there is no proven alternative to silicon-based computing. So far, there are four distinct contenders. None has proven itself yet and only one has parentage in the science of biology.

*Optical computing,* instead of using electrons across wires, uses photons to carry data along laser light beams. Optical transistors have been built and have the advantage that photons can pass by one another without interference, but the pieces that make the box are large and awkward to use.

*Quantum computing* bounces a laser or radio beam off spinning atomic nuclei. It uses the direction of the axis on which individual atoms spin to do its calculations; up or down is equivalent to 0 or 1. Remember, code is code. It is important to linking information and biotechnologies that, at the quantum level, inorganic and organic behave the same way, again suggesting a potential bridge between information and bio-economies. Such computers would be the ultimate in tiny and powerful, but they are also the most unstable and can be crashed by just an errant cosmic ray.

*Molecular computing* or moletronics replaces silicon transistors with molecules as the tiny switches and logic gates. So far elusive, this design would bridge chemistry and electrical engineering. Workable models do not yet exist, but a Hewlett-Packard scientist has mused that "These things are small enough that you could stir them into paint and cover a wall with them . . . (However), there's a significant software problem in getting this paint to communicate and self-organize" (Moletronics will change everything, *Wired*, July 2000, pp. 240–251). When they are that small, they could embed zillions of black boxes in the skin of an airplane, instead of just two in the cockpit and also zillions in the body of the doctor's patient.

*DNA computing* is the front runner for the organic solution to more powerful computing. DNA computing uses those four nucleic acids of the genes' double helix (C, G, A and T). The solutions are located on the series of base pairs of the helical strands. Existing nanotechnology makes features approximately 100 nanometers in size, whereas the space between the letters in the genetic code are only 0.34 nanometers. Nature crams much more information into much less space. The DNA computing method has been proven but has also been unwieldy to build. DNA works best in wet not solid form and does not conduct electricity well, which may limit its direct use in electronic devices.

DNA computing should not be confused with biochips, which

place and measure some organic functioning on silicon chips. Affymetrix, for example, is building silicon chips embedded with DNA that can test for 6000 genetic conditions and this will soon reach 400,000 conditions. However, while biochips are majorly important for an information bridge that combines the inorganic and organic, they do not resolve the processing power problem. If biochips continue to get better and cheaper, this hybrid might find uses well beyond the life sciences industries and they could serve as an interim computational platform until a truly new processing design is practical.

To conclude, the key to the economy of the future lies in its deep structure. And, whether this structure is rooted in information technology or biotechnology, in optical, quantum, molecular, or DNA computing, in inorganic silicon microprocessors or organic biochips, they are all code based and they all work from the bottom up.

# 20

## Beyond 2020

### How can we accept evolution

### yet believe that it stops with us?

This is probably one of the most philosophical pieces I have written. It is my take on why and how, as a species, we will not have the final say on life. It seems like an appropriate note the end this book on. *Lesson from the Future:* how can we accept evolution yet believe that it stops with us?

By the time we enter the bio-economy, we will have accomplished the blending of genetics and computers. This blending will take us in two very different directions: one will be biological and deeper inside ourselves, the other will be chemical and much further away in time and space.

Turning inward, the bio-economy will see carbon-based organic substances that function like semiconductors. Computers will enter the body, not like pacemakers and hearing aids that are patched in, but – through microtechnology – like cells that are absorbed and integrated into our bodies. Remember that 90 percent of the cells we call "us" do not have our genes. Microtechnology will add a few more. Scientists do not yet know what a molecular computer will look like, although places like Carnegie-Mellon University have opened centers for molecular electronics. Still, many cringe at words like "biochips" because they raise expectations far in excess of near-term reality. Prototype memories have been predicted for several years but, like the bio-economy itself, have still not arrived.

Turning outward, the bio-economy will also see silicon-based inorganic substances that have some brain-like functions. In future economies, we will pass more and more qualities that we ascribe to organic "life" onto non-organic creations that exist outside our bodies. But are computers the next life form? Dr Robert Jastrow, the founder of NASA's Goddard Institute, reaches this conclusion in his fascinating investigation into the evolution of intelligence on earth: "The era of carbon-chemistry life is drawing to a close on the earth and a new era of silicon-based life – indestructible, immortal, infinitely expandable – is beginning." In the long term, scientists like Jastrow may be right, but we believe that such an age is many economies away, not in the next one.

Others may be closer to the mark. Roger Penrose, for example, the Oxford mathematician and co-researcher with the famed Stephen Hawking, believes that quantum phenomena are likely to be of importance in the operation of the brain. While he thinks that one day they may explain qualities such as intuition, judgement, and emotions, he views these as attributes of humans and animals, not of computers.

The computing power of today's neural networks is still less than that of a cockroach, let alone an animal or human. In the coming together of genetics and computers, therefore, the brain-like analogy is not in terms of scale but in terms of the way that information is processed using neurocomputers. Computer memories will have more than enough capacity to capture and store as much information as can the human brain. The task for technoloy beyond the 2020s will be in how the information is processed. In the middle distance, between molecules and stars, the technology of the brain will be one route to our distant future.

The route to the bio-economy will be the micro-route through genetic engineering. Our travels to economies and worlds even further beyond, however, may well be the macro-route of evolutionary engineering. For this, we would have to remove ourselves from the center of things. Then, we might marvel at an extraordinary participation in our own evolutionary futures. Many balk at the notion of non-carbon life. They ask, "how can the ineffable qualities of humans be passed on, into computers?" In return, however, we must ask, "how can we accept evolution yet believe that it stops with us?"

If it does not stop with us and we accept the evolution of beings more intelligent than ourselves, where do they come from? If species do not spring into existence *de novo*, but evolve from earlier forms, then might not humans evolve forms more intelligent than themselves? We seem to think that the apes did it. Are we not at least as capable as they were of such a creative bootstrapping act? If we admit to this line of speculative reasoning, then we should look to current scientific and technological advances for the likely forms of our future businesses, our future economies, and perhaps even our future ancestors.

# Notes

## Chapter 2

1. Kevin Kelly, *Out of Control* (Reading, MA: Addison-Wesley, 1994), p. 185.

## Chapter 3

1. Frances Cairncross, *The Death of Distance* (Boston, MA: Harvard Business School Press, 1997).

## Chapter 5

1. Jeff Donn, "6 Percent Are Web Addicts," Associated Press Online, 23 August 1999.
2. US Department of Commerce, *Statistical Abstract of the United States:1975* (Washington, DC: Government Printing Office, 1975); US Department of Commerce, *Statistical Abstract of the United States: 1977* (Washington, DC: Government Printing Office, 1977); *Economic Report of the President* (Washington, DC: Government Printing office, 1975, 1991, 1999).
3. S&P Market Insight, Industry Report: Computers "Hardware" (S&P data from IDC) and S&P Market Insight Industry Report; Industry Name: Computers (Software & Services) Computers: Commercial Services Industry Survey, July 1999.
4. Louis Uchitelle, "Greenspan Ties Debate on Rates to the Markets," *New*

*York Times*, 28 August 1999. Copyright © by the New York Times Co. Reprinted by permission.

5. Authors'calculation from data from OneSource Global Business Browser, 9 November 1999, <http://globalbb.onesource.com>, using data provided by Market Guide, Info. US and Corp. Tech.

6. Internal Revenue Service, <97inprel.exe at http://www.irs.gov/tax-stats/ soi/soi_bul.html>. The statistical increase understates the importance of investments, because it does not include unrealized capital gains from from tax-deferred retirement assets.

7. Investment Company Institute, *Mutual Funds Factbook* 1999 (Washington, DC: Investment Company Institute,1999). Also available at <wwwici.org/aboutfunds/factbook toc.html>.

8. "Worker Capitalist," *Wall Street Journal*, 30 November 1999.

## Chapter 6

1. Board of Governors of the Federal Reserve System, *Flow of Funds Accounts of the United States Flows and Outstandings Second Quarter: 1999* (Washington, DC: Government Printing Office, 1999); Board of Governors of the Federal Reserve System, *Flow of Funds Coded Tables 20 September, 1994* (Washington, DC: Government Printing Office, 1994).

2. "Investors, Unite," from *A Survey of Fund Management, 25* October 1997, 3. © 1997 The Economist Newspaper Group, Inc. Reprinted with permission. Further reproduction prohibited. <www.economist.com>.

3. US Bureau of the Census, *Measuring 50 Years of Economic Change Using the March Current Population* Survey, Current Population Reports, P60-203 (Washington, DC: Government Printing Office, 1998), C20.

4. Robert Lenzner and Stephen S. Johnson, "Seeing Things as They Really Are," 10 March 1997, <http://wwwforbes.com/forbes/97/0310/ 5905122a.htm> (11 November 1999).

5. Kevin Kelly, "Wealth Is Overrated," *Wired* 6.03, March 1998. © The Condé Nast Publications Inc. All rights reserved. Reprinted by permission.

6. Bill Gates, with Nathan Myhrvold and Peter Rinearson, *The Road Ahead* (New York: Viking, 1995), 58.

7. Roxana Frost (speech presented at Ernst & Young's Measuring the Future Conference, Cambridge, Mass., 27 October 1999).

8. Katie Hafner, "Common Ground Elusive as Technology Have-Nots Meet Haves," *New York Times,* 8 July 1999.

9. John Stackhouse, "Village Phones Ring Up Profit: CELL-PHONE CRAZE," *The Globe and Mail,* 6 July 1998.

10. Tom Neubig, Gautam Jaggi and Robin Lee, *Chapter 7 Bankruptcy Petitioners' Repayment Ability Under H.R. 833: The National Perspective* (Washington, DC: Ernst & Young LLP, 1999). Also available at <http://wwweycom/ publicate/eyecon/pdf/reportgg.pdf?? (1 November1999).

11. Stackhouse, "Village Phones Ring Up Profit."

12. "A Look at the Balance Sheet," <http://wwwgrameen-info.org/bank/lookbs.html> (11 November 1999).
13. United Nations Economic Commission for Africa, *Economic Report on Afiica 1999: The Challenges of Poverty Reduction and Sustainability*, United Nations, <http://wwwun.org/Depts/eca/divis/espd/ecrepgg.htm> (9 September 1999).

## Chapter 12

1. The Egyptians used slavery and the Romans conscription to accumulate capital. We're just Eurocentric here for illustrative purposes.
2. The fact that three books by the name *Intellectual Capital* all came out within a three-month period in 1997 is one indication of the pervasiveness of this idea. The three are by Tom Stewart, a member of Fortune's senior board of editors; Leif Edvinsson and Michael Malone (Edvinsson is director of Intellectual Capital at Skandia, a Swedish-based insurance firm, and Malone is an accomplished business journalist); and Annie Brookitig, a UK-based consultant.
3. Again, we are not attempting a full economic history. Many institutional changes facilitated the rise of debt-to-equity ratios.
4. Yugi Ijiri, *Momentum Accounting and Triple-Entry Booking* (American Accounting Association, 1989).

## Chapter 14

1. Robert Lenzner and Stephen S. Johnson, "Seeing Things as They Really Are," 10 March 1997, <http://www.forbes.com/forbes/97/031@/5905i22a.htm> (11 November 1999).
2. Larry Downes and Chunka Mui, *Unleashing the Killer App: Digital Strategies for Market Dominance* (Boston: Harvard Business School Press, 1998).
3. Jeffrey Taylor, CEO of Monster.com, telephone interview with Christopher Meyer and Christoph Knoess, Cambridge, Mass., 9 June 1999.
4. John Kao, *Jamming: The Art and Discipline of Business Creativity* (New York: HarperBusiness, 1997).

# Index